SOUTHERN RAILWAY
MISCELLANY

A much-lamented route is that from Havant across Langstone Harbour to Hayling Island. Here the reason for closure was stated to be threefold — limited revenue, the state of the timber bridge linking the island with the mainland, and the age of the Class A1X 'Terriers' — the only locomotives permitted on the line. No 32678 is seen on the bridge in 1962, the last full year of operation. *J. Scrace*

SOUTHERN RAILWAY
MISCELLANY

Kevin Robertson

WHITEWAY'S
WINES &
DEVON CYDER

OPC

An imprint of
Ian Allan Publishing

Contents

First published 2003

ISBN 0 86093 582 5

All rights reserved. No part of this book may be reproduced or transmitted in any form or by any means, electronic or mechanical, including photocopying, recording or by any information storage and retrieval system, without permission from the Publisher in writing.

© Kevin Robertson 2003

Published by Oxford Publishing Co

an imprint of Ian Allan Publishing Ltd, Hersham, Surrey KT12 4RG.
Printed by Ian Allan Printing Ltd, Hersham, Surrey KT12 4RG.

Code: 0304/A2

Title page:
The approaches to Waterloo in the mid-1960s, with a rebuilt Light Pacific and 4-SUB unit passing in opposite directions. *Ian Allan Library*

Left:
The single-road depot at Okehampton. Built of concrete blocks with an asbestos roof, this building dated from *c*1920 and replaced an earlier wooden structure which had been destroyed by fire. Primarily intended for servicing and turning visiting engines, including those working ballast trains from the nearby Meldon Quarry, from 1947 the depot had a 70ft turntable and was thus able to deal with the larger types of locomotive, such as the Light Pacific seen here. *Stephenson Locomotive Society*

Right:
Think of the Southern and the image conjured may well be that of green electric stock or maybe an unrebuilt 'Bulleid' slipping away from a start. There was, of course, far more to the system than that; it was, after all, a railway where suburban and branch-line services intermingled and over which the tentacles of electrification would eventually spread far and wide. Here, at the start of our photographic tribute, is the branch-line idyll: Cowes on a lazy afternoon, with No W29 resting after bringing in a train from Newport. *Ian Allan Library*

Introduction

Smallest of the four pre-nationalisation companies, the Southern Railway was unique in Britain in that its dominance was in passenger services rather than freight, in relation to revenue. It could not compete with the LMS and LNER with regard to distance, although against the GWR, its earlier long-term adversary, the Southern could hold its head high, with its principal services running as far west as Exeter. After that it may have been a slightly different story, although, to be fair, neither had an ideal solution for serving the western extremities of Devon and thence Cornwall, the GWR hampered by the fearsome gradients west of Newton Abbot and the SR by its tortuous route skirting Dartmoor.

Elsewhere the SR had shown it was a railway well able to serve the community. Its forté had to be two-fold: the centres of population it was able to serve and then the limited distances necessary to reach the coastal locations so favoured by the masses. In this way considerable revenue was earned by transporting the masses to and from their places of work in the capital, whilst the coastal towns of Kent, Sussex, Hampshire and Dorset provided much traffic in the form of day-trippers and holidaymakers — a situation that resulted in duplicate trains, often affording standing-room only, right up to the early 1960s.

The above is but a brief *précis* of the make-up and development of a system which began piecemeal in the 1830s and '40s with lines from London eastwards to the Kent coast, south to Brighton and southwest to Southampton. The original intention was also to serve Bristol — the reason the Southampton route travelled west as far as Basingstoke before turning sharply south. As is well known, that idea was still-born, the merchants of Bristol dissatisfied with the idea of being served by a 'branch' and instead favouring the vision of a young engineer named Brunel… . This is not to say that the companies which would amalgamate to form the SR had no notables of their own; they did, Joseph Locke and Thomas Brassey being two examples, even if such names are less well-known outside the annals of railway history.

The avowed intention of all the early concerns was to provide lines to serve areas where revenue was likely to be attracted. In some cases there was also encouragement locally, merchants and traders seeing the prospect of cheaper transport of goods to wider markets and thus increased profits. Make no mistake: whilst the profit was seen as the principal objective, the public service would come much later. Likewise the first railways were conceived primarily with the movement of goods as paramount. Government would also encourage a connection with the dockyard at Portsmouth, so as to avoid the longer and potentially dangerous sea journey around the Sussex and Kent coasts before being able to reach the comparative safety of the Thames Estuary. In the early part of the 19th century, recent wars with France were still uppermost in the minds of many.

As time passed and the first goals were achieved, efforts were directed towards identifying additional locations deserving of a service. Later still would come further connections and branch lines, many of these starting off as independent concerns, keen to become linked to the railway map yet perhaps having originally scorned the idea of a connection. The paradox a century or so later is with the new Channel Tunnel Rail Link being built from London. Years earlier the towns along the new routes would encourage the railway to deviate towards their community and provide a station and facilities; now the wheel has turned full circle,

Back to the main line, and a scene showing the Southern in its final days of private ownership: 'Merchant Navy' class 4-6-2 No 21C2 *Union Castle* approaches Salisbury with an up express. On the left is one of two LSWR signalboxes in the area which operated the points and signals by pneumatic means. *Ian Allan Library*

and the general attitude is one of 'not in my back yard!'. Hindsight, of course, is a wonderful thing, and it is inappropriate to compare 21st-century situations with those applying 150 or so years ago. Suffice it to say that, had the requirements of today been envisaged all that time ago, a very different system would have emerged. As it is, the system of today is desperately attempting to provide a service based on a 19th-century network. In an ideal world we would rip it up and start again.

Away, though, from the politics and pontifications, and a return to the infrastructure and engineering. The relatively easy terrain of southern England meant that the engineers — and shareholders — were spared many of the difficulties encountered elsewhere. But this is not to say there were none, and the greatest obstacle, affecting both LBSCR and LSWR, was the chalk barrier of the South Downs, which run from East Sussex to central Hampshire. Accordingly there was a need for major construction, in the form of cuttings, viaducts and tunnels, sufficient to delay completion of the London & Southampton main line — later the LSWR — between Winchester and Basingstoke for some two years; either side of Andover Road (later Micheldever) there were four tunnels,

as well as embankments and cuttings of almost 100ft. To the east, the nominally independent Mid Hants Railway Co, whose line from Alton to Winchester had opened in the 1860s, avoided heavy engineering by simply going up one side and down the other, but this resulted in fearsome 1-in-60 gradients either side of the station at Medstead & Four Marks, as well as giving this part of the railway its nickname of 'over the Alps'. The 'Portsmouth Direct' line from Guildford south through Petersfield to Havant was another where major engineering had been called for, explaining why it too arrived later on the scene, allied to which there was considerable conflict with the LBSCR at Havant, more of which anon.

Arguably the most heavily engineered route for the least return was that through the Meon Valley from Alton to Fareham, opened as late as 1903. Its very existence has always been the subject of debate, and, indeed, a century later there is still no clear explanation as to its construction or intended use. The area between Alton and Fareham was sparsely populated agricultural land, with no sizeable centres of population for nearly 10 miles either side of what became the intermediate stations — doubtless the reason the early railway promoters had ignored the area. A route in the form of an independent concern could perhaps have been understood, albeit one where investment would have been almost guaranteed no return. Instead this was a line promoted by the LSWR itself — 22 miles of heavily engineered railway with two long tunnels and a massive viaduct, the major works of which were even intended to take a double track, with relatively easy gradients for most of the route. For whom, then, and for what purpose was such a line built? To service and open up the local area? Hardly. To keep out the GWR? Possible, but unlikely; the GWR had already reached Basingstoke, and if it had wanted a connection to the South Coast that opportunity had existed since the 1880s with the Didcot, Newbury & Southampton line, which terminated at Winchester. To provide a better service to the towns of Fareham and Gosport? Possible also; perhaps the intention was to develop Stokes Bay (near Gosport) as the principal staging-point for the ferry service to the Isle of Wight. Certainly it was the shortest crossing-point of the Solent, with a railway connection as far as the bay already in existence. In this way too the LSWR could have obtained the lion's share of receipts (owning, as it did, the whole route), without having to share with the LBSCR. Or was it built simply to safeguard access to Portsmouth, should relations with the LBSCR turn sour?

Portsmouth had long been seen as a prize, naval traffic, in the form of men, equipment and victualling, being eagerly sought by both LBSCR and LSWR. But to reach the port the LBSCR line had to follow the coast as far as Arundel before turning northeast to run through the heart of Sussex and then eventually Redhill. The situation as far as the LSWR was concerned was equally convoluted, its main line being accessible only by means of a journey northwest to Eastleigh. Portsmouth traffic was handled under a 'pooling' arrangement — an uneasy truce existing between the players. Small wonder, then, that Portsmouth was ripe for improved communication, hence the promotion and construction of the aforementioned 'Portsmouth Direct' route, which included a connection with the LBSCR main line just east of Havant and running powers thence for the final few miles onto Portsea Island. (The peninsula on which Portsmouth had developed is surrounded by water. The area is naturally tidal and, were it not for bridges, would be cut off at varying times each day.)

With the completion of the LSWR's new line from Guildford, the LBSCR realised its share of London traffic would fall dramatically; hence, having failed to halt the new line in Parliament, it attempted to do so on site at Havant. The result was a stand-off between workers loyal to each company which could have resulted in a fearsome fight. Fortunately common sense prevailed, and the LBSCR, knowing the situation was hopeless, conceded, the two companies maintaining a shared interest in the area until both ceased to exist in 1923. This sharing had one slightly amusing side-effect involving the working of the line from Fratton to East Southsea from 1885. Built to compete with the city's street trams, it was operated alternate years by each company — on 31 December the staff would collect their bags and leave, the replacement men arriving the next day and working the railway until the same time the next year!

Manual labour on the main line, near Brookwood, with not an orange jacket in sight! The conductor rail is being slewed into its approximate position, in connection with the 1937 extension of electrification to Farnham and Alton. *British Railways*

But to return finally to the *raison d'être* of the Meon Valley route. In 1903 such difficulties as had occurred at Havant were decades past, and conflicts of such type were generally unknown. Did the LSWR feel its monopoly was still threatened? For whatever reason the Meon Valley line started and remained an enigma. Its services poorly patronised from the outset, and revenue never matching running costs, the line did well to survive as late as 1955, although in the interim the Southern had already effected economies. Ironically it remains today a drain on resources, as the successors to the Southern and BR remain responsible for the maintenance of safety on the two tunnels at Privett and West Meon, despite the fact that the line will soon have been closed for longer than it was open.

If ferry services to the Isle of Wight were a consideration at Portsmouth, those to France and Belgium were a consideration further east, with the LBSCR spending considerable sums on development of the port at Newhaven.

The result was a passenger and freight service to Dieppe, although the majority of trade across the Channel was handled by the SECR further around the coast, from Folkestone, Dover and (later) Ramsgate. Here, railway-operated steamers plied a regular service across the Channel, and at that time, such travel involved passport controls. Even so, it was a buoyant and booming business, the SECR ensuring services to/from the ports were given priority over its other traffic, although weather conditions could often delay the sailings, with consequent knock-on effects elsewhere on the system.

At the opposite end of the Southern the LSWR maintained an interest in the marine operations at Southampton and Plymouth, Weymouth at that time being the province of the GWR. At Plymouth there was the Ocean Liner passenger service, whilst at Southampton, under the guidance of LSWR General Manager Sir Herbert Walker, the railway was quick to recognise the potential for growth from the docks and invested heavily in their development and expansion. This investment would continue apace for some years, with vast areas of waterfront being reclaimed, often using spoil excavated from railway property. Thus space was cleared for the sidings at Micheldever, whilst by the 1930s Southampton Docks would be among the largest and most modern within the UK, used by ocean-going services to and from the far corners of the globe.

On the passenger front, steam reigned supreme until basically the end of the 19th century, but the first steps towards an alternative — in the form of electricity — were already being considered. The advantages of electric traction had been demonstrated elsewhere, both on the tube lines and abroad, whilst the ever-increasing suburban traffic led the

management of the railway companies seriously to investigate an alternative to steam. While the lines south of the Thames were not alone in the transportation of commuter traffic, what they did have was probably the greatest density, and it made sense to seek alternatives sooner than would be considered elsewhere. Two schemes were investigated — a 660V direct-current system from a conductor rail alongside the running lines and a 6.7kV alternating current from overhead wires. The latter was favoured by the LBSCR, and installation of the necessary lineside equipment commenced on the South London line so that services were able to begin. The LSWR, however, preferred the former scheme, and, although the disadvantage was primarily that of exposure from a safety perspective, it considered the saving (compared with the overhead) advantageous, whilst a further primary consideration was the speed with which the conductor rail could be installed. Following the Grouping in 1923, the LSWR's prominence in electrification matters meant that the third-rail system was chosen for development and the overhead slowly abandoned.

By the 1930s the tentacles of electrification had extended to cover most of the suburban lines. The next stage was an extension into the countryside, and accordingly Brighton and Portsmouth received their electric services before the outbreak of war in 1939. Brighton had been an obvious choice, being just an hour from Victoria, the new service including a Pullman train, the still lamented 'Brighton Belle'. No such luxury was afforded Portsmouth, although new stock was provided which included units with destination number covering what would normally be the right-hand window of the cab, giving them a 'one-eyed' appearance; not surprisingly, they quickly gained the nickname of 'Nelsons'. The steepish gradients on the 'Portsmouth Direct' line had

Several pairs of eyes watch the operation of the lift allowing tube stock from 'The Drain' — the Waterloo & City line — to be sent to and retrieved from the sub-surface line. In 1948 an ''M7' 0-4-4T had the misfortune to fall down the shaft and had to be cut up *in situ. J. H. Meredith*

made it an obvious choice for electrification, and by now Portsmouth also had electric services along the coast to Brighton and via the mid-Sussex route through Arundel. This would be the extent of main-line electrification prewar, although it is likely that Folkestone, Dover and the Kent Coast would soon have been dealt with, with Bournemouth next, had conflict not ensued. Whether Salisbury and the West of England would have followed remains doubtful, however, as it is unlikely that traffic volumes would have been sufficient to warrant such investment beyond the Wiltshire city.

Electrification would recommence with the Kent Coast scheme in 1957, the Bournemouth line following a decade later. Even so, there were still gaps; indeed, the line from Basingstoke to Salisbury has still not been electrified and seems unlikely to be for the foreseeable future.

Throughout the life of the Southern Railway, then, steam would reign supreme on the longer-distance routes, although, aside from those to Exeter and beyond, no journey took much more than two hours. Pullman services were also provided, to Brighton, and later there would be a 'Kentish Belle', a 'Bournemouth Belle' and a 'Devon Belle', the latter including an observation coach. Freight also continued to be almost 100% steam-worked, as did branch lines. Steam would also survive on the numerous empty-coach workings from Waterloo, where the intensity of the electric service made such workings difficult for crews and controllers.

Electrification brought disadvantages as well as advantages, the Southern becoming a victim of its own success, in that the popularity of the swish new electrics meant traffic volumes increased to such an extent that overcrowding became a problem. The situation was exacerbated by the considerable suburban housing programme then underway in what had previously been greenfield sites; to serve what had become 'semi-detached' London, new stations were provided in the 'art deco' style of the period.

Another downside to the massive investment in modern traction was that the design of new steam locomotives was allowed to take a back seat. CME Richard Maunsell was approaching retirement, and, whilst his designs were functional, the impetus on new design and development had waned; accordingly, with the solitary exception of his remarkable 'Schools' class, the initiative in terms of steam technology had definitely passed to Crewe and Doncaster. It would be left to a new man (a product of the LNER) to rectify matters; Oliver Bulleid's approach was that (almost) nothing was sacrosanct, with well-known results. Regrettably history would not allow all his ideas to come to fruition, and it is doubtful whether Bulleid ever had the opportunity to develop his true potential. What did emerge, in the shape of the 'Merchant Navy', 'West Country', 'Q1' and 'Leader' classes, demonstrated the fertile brain of a man genuinely intending to revolutionise and improve the steam services and the lot of the crews. That not all of those objectives were achieved is more the result of outside situations over which he had no control, although the converse argument is that, given the conditions, he should have adopted a more traditional approach.

It is tempting to pretend that the Southern's route mileage remained constant or even increased during private ownership and that Beeching, the enthusiasts' demon, was a product solely of the BR era. In truth, the Southern was

The unique 6-TC set which was formed around the time of the Bournemouth electrification as a stopgap to cover a temporary shortage of passenger rolling stock capable of 'push-pull' working. Seen here in company with Class 33 No D6580, possibly in late 1965 when first formed, it was destined to be short-lived, so photographs are somewhat rare. *Ian Allan Library*

perhaps yet more ruthless, even if hardly reported as such at the time. There was no room for sentiment where shareholders were concerned, old stock being withdrawn and lines closed as necessary. The biggest such programme had occurred in the early 1930s, the situation not assisted by the general economic conditions of the period, as described earlier. In addition economies were made elsewhere, redundant or little-used track and signals being recovered for re-use, although perhaps most surprising at the time was the retention of the various routes west of Exeter. Not without reason were the lines of Devon and Cornwall referred to as the 'Withered Arm', while someone at Waterloo is quoted as saying that it would be a help if Paddington could be made to take over these lines itself. This was probably something of a tongue-in-cheek remark, although the difficulties facing the Southern in the area were real enough. True, in the summer months loadings (and thus receipts) could be high, but the season could be short — holidays were nowhere near as long as they are today, and for the rest of the year lightly patronised trains traversed the same expensive-to-maintain lines, and station staff still occupied their stations and needed to be paid. It would be left to the aforementioned Beeching to deal with the situation, although in truth he was purely a figurehead for the organisation, and, had it not been he, then someone else would have wielded the axe — possibly in a yet more ruthless manner.

The economic situation facing the Southern in the 1920s and '30s had not been helped by increasing competition from the roads. Coach travel was emerging as an alternative for passenger traffic, whilst the private carrier was also starting to tempt away goods. For the first time, then, there was a credible threat to revenue, and it was up to every department to attempt to redress the balance. One way this was achieved was in John Elliot's publicity from Waterloo. A series of posters was introduced, one of which (featuring the small boy peering up at the engine driver) has justifiably been recognised as a classic in its own right. Publicity was given to almost every aspect of operation, from the benefits of holidays and visits to the cities, towns and various coastal destinations served, through to Camping Coach holidays, foreign travel, living in the suburban area, and to luggage in advance, season tickets and the like. Unfortunately all publicity is not necessarily good publicity, and the accidents at Sevenoaks in 1927 and Woking in 1947 brought about the type of coverage that was definitely not wanted.

Steam and electric would continue to operate in close harmony until July 1967, after which BR's new corporate image gradually took over. This book offers a glimpse of the Southern prior to that date — a time when the majority of holidays were still taken by train, and when passengers regarded the odd smut in the eye as an acceptable part of rail travel.

SECR locomotives

Above:
Having seemingly ignored the former SECR so far, it is time to redress the balance, with what is probably an official view of 'D' class 4-4-0 No 736 in superb condition — one can almost imagine the smart lined-green livery. The locomotive is posed with a rake of six Pullman cars — two Third-class, two Firsts, a Second and a final Third — on what may well have been a 'Club' service. *Ian Allan Library*

Below:
The diminutive 'P' class 0-6-0T was another former South Eastern design, being instantly recognisable as such from the shape of the cab roof. As with the Brighton 'Terrier', the short wheelbase and light weight made the type ideal for working over lightly laid branches and also in sidings where sharp curves abounded. No 31323, dating from 1910, was recorded at Shoreham on 20 August 1952. *E. R. Wethersett*

The SECR, itself a working union of the South Eastern and London, Chatham & Dover companies, contributed a number of 4-4-0s, including 'F1' No A197, which had been built at Ashford Works in 1890. It was rebuilt in the style shown here in 1916 and lasted in service until 1933. *Tony Sedgwick collection*

Another example of an ex-SECR 4-4-0 — this time 'B1' No 1021, coupled to articulated set No 514 at Leysdown. Built at Ashford in 1899, this locomotive survived to the very end of the Southern Railway, being withdrawn in 1947. *Tony Sedgwick collection*

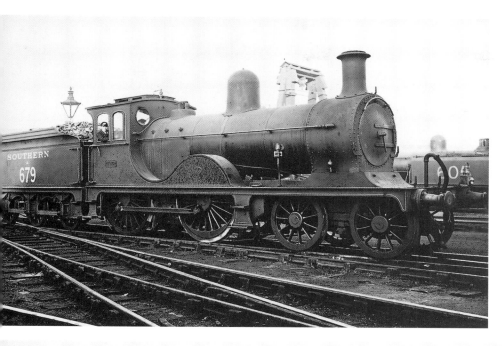

An acute shortage of locomotives in 1900 led the SECR to take over five 4-4-0s built for the Great North of Scotland Railway by Neilson Reid in 1899. Designed by Pickersgill, all five survived basically unaltered throughout their lives. The first withdrawal took place in 1925, with the last of the group going just two years later. No A679, seen here at Battersea, remained in service until 1926. *Tony Sedgwick collection*

The South Eastern also possessed a number of 0-4-4 tank engines, including the 'Q' class, a number of which were rebuilt to Class Q1. No A237, in original condition, is seen at St Leonards at the end of July 1926; it was withdrawn from service by the end of the year. *H. C. Casserley / Tony Sedgwick collection*

Size doesn't matter. One of the diminutive but famed LBSCR 'Terriers', No B635, inside Fratton roundhouse in 1946. Engines of this class were some of the longest-lived of all steam types, No B635 having been built back in 1878 as LBSCR No 35 *Morden*. They were first used on London suburban services, but, following electrification, they were more commonly employed on branch lines, although they were also ideal as works shunters. Having been rebuilt to 'A1X' in 1922, the locomotive seen here was taken into departmental use as 377S in 1946 and renumbered DS377 in February 1958. It returned to general use less than a year later in January 1959, this time as No 32635 and was eventually withdrawn in March 1963 at the ripe old age of 85.
Tony Sedgwick collection

LBSCR locomotives

Another engine whose origins were on the former LBSCR system was Stroudley 'D1' class 0-4-2T No B298. The letter 'B' (visible above the number) was an SR-instigated identification as to its origins on the Brighton section.
Ian Allan Library

The Southern inherited a number of large tank types from the former LBSCR, one of which was the 'I1' class. Rebuilt by Maunsell with a 'B4' boiler, these locomotives were re-designated 'I1X'. No B596 is depicted in ex-works condition at Brighton. *Ian Allan Library*

The 'I3s' were similar to the 'I1s' but were constructed with larger wheels for fast passenger work. Heavier trains and then electrification displaced these smart machines from front-line duties, although they survived for some time on lesser workings. No 2021 is seen here at Brighton *Ian Allan Library*

Class H1 No 2039 *Hartland Point*, stabled between duties sometime in the 1930s. Introduced in 1905 for use on the fast Victoria–Brighton services, these Atlantics were displaced by electrification in the 1930s and found a new role on the coastal services between Brighton and Bournemouth — duties they would continue to perform until well into the 1950s. *Ian Allan Library*

'H1' No 2040 *St. Catherine's Point* leaves Chichester on the last leg of a special from London Bridge to Portsmouth on 17 April 1938. The headcode discs indicated to the signalman the route the train was taking rather than (as with the other railway companies) the class of the train, while 'SPL' on the upper disc signified that this was an additional (rather than a regular timetabled) working. *K. O. B. Nichols*

The LBSCR's affinity for large tank engines is demonstrated here to advantage in the form of 'J1' class 4-6-2T No 2325, originally No 325 *Abergavenny* — the name was removed by the Southern in April 1924. Built at Brighton in 1910, No 325 and sister engine No 326 were used initially on fast main-line services to Victoria; after electrification of the Brighton line they appeared on a variety of services, although principally still within the former LBSCR area. Wartime saw both engines travel further afield, including onto the South Western section, and they would survive into BR ownership, being taken out of service and broken up in 1951. *Ian Allan Library*

The largest of all the Brighton tank engines were L. Billinton's seven 'L' class Baltics, built at intervals between 1914 and 1922. One of these managed to retain its name in SR days, this being No B333 *Remembrance*, dedicated to the memory of railwaymen killed in World War 1. Following electrification of the Brighton and Eastbourne lines in the 1930s all seven were rebuilt as 4-6-0 tender engines (the tenders coming from 'S15' class 4-6-0s) and as such remained in service until replaced by new BR Standard designs in the mid-1950s. *Ian Allan Library*

The LSWR's locomotive supremo in the 1870s was W. G. Beattie, whose designs were functional if perhaps lacking somewhat in external grace. As per the proverb, however, one should 'never judge a book by its cover', for 0-6-0ST No 330 of 1876 was both functional and efficient. This locomotive survived (just) into SR days, not being withdrawn until December 1924. *Ian Allan Library*

LSWR locomotives

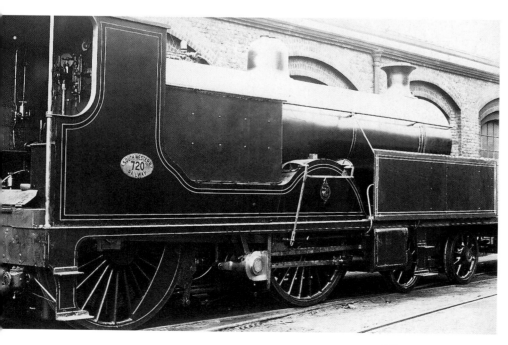

Seeing the LSWR from the 19th into the 20th century was Dugald Drummond, a Scotsman with a fearsome reputation — and a beard to match! Whilst Drummond was without doubt a capable engineer, he seemed sometimes to veer towards the eccentric, as witness here with his 4-2-2-0 design. This is No 720 as re-boilered in 1905, the intention being to increase efficiency with the use of firebox cross-tubes. The idea was perfect; in practice, the additional maintenance necessary easily outweighed any advantage gained. The presence of the indicator shelter, and at that time even this was lined out, meant that trials had been, or were about to be carried out. *Ian Allan Library*

On the South Western, as it was known, the designs of William Adams were to survive well into Southern days. Some of his machines were arguably the most graceful ever to run in Great Britain. (I await the brickbats …!) This is Adams '460' class 4-4-0 No 526 of 1887, built by Robert Stephenson and shown at the 1888 Newcastle Exhibition, where it was awarded a Gold Medal — hence the plaque on the cabside. This engine also worked the first train over the new direct line to Bournemouth via Sway in 1888.
Ian Allan Library

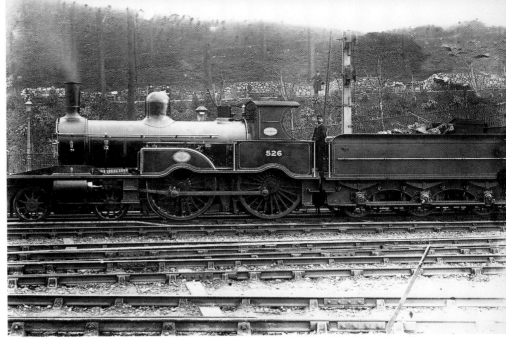

Another of the same class — this time No 469, dating from 1884 — outside what is believed to be Eastleigh shed. From this angle the elegant lines are exemplified, although it is doubtful whether æsthetics were at the forefront of the designer's mind. Despite their appearance, the earlier and smaller, Adams 4-4-0s were soon outclassed as trains' weights and speeds increased, and all were out of use by 1929, No 469 going in April 1927.
Ian Allan Library

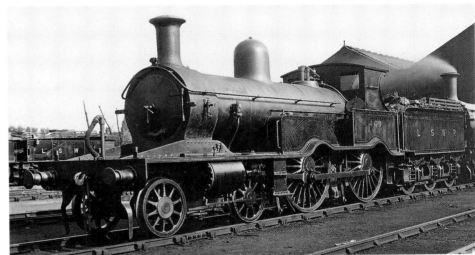

Another 0-4-4T class originating on the LSWR was the 'T1' design, all of which would be withdrawn very soon after nationalisation. This example, No 367, is shown at Eastleigh sometime in the late 1930s on a GWR working from Winchester Chesil to Southampton.
Tony Sedgwick collection

Another 0-4-4T, this time a Class O2, and, judging from its smart condition, one which has recently been outshopped from works. No 231 was a Western-section locomotive — hence the 'E' above the number — built in December 1894 and would last in service until February 1953. *Ian Allan Library*

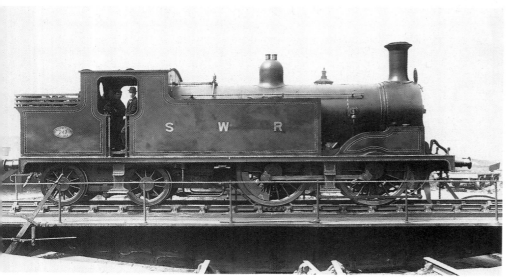

Having criticised Drummond, it is also only fair to acknowledge that, in his 'T9', '700' and 'M7' classes, he produced engines that were equal to any other of the period; indeed examples of all three designs would remain in service until the 1960s. This is 'M7' No 247 at Nine Elms, showing the first type of lettering used on the class and also the cast numberplate. What price today at auction for this relic? *Ian Allan Library*

Notwithstanding the success of the 'M7', Drummond's successor, Robert Urie, sought to improve the efficiency of the class, fitting No 126 with a superheater which resulted in an extended smokebox being required. The alteration did little to improve its looks, however, and no further members of the class were so treated as it was said to be unsteady at speed. Another change typical of Urie was the fitting of clamps to the lower half of the smokebox door. *Ian Allan Library*

With goods traffic a lesser priority than passengers, the Southern had no need for numerous locomotives specially designed for such work, and most engines served a dual role. This is No 316 of the former LSWR '700' class (also referred to as 'Black Motors'), seen at Byfleet junction on what is a local or a transfer goods from the London area terminating at Woking. *E. R. Wethersett*

Demoted from main-line duties, Adams 'A12' No 618 is seen while in use on local freight work in the Guildford area in 1947. It is doubtful whether it lived up to its chalked nickname of 'Ye Flying Saucer'. The locomotive was destined to last just one more year, being withdrawn in 1948. *Tony Sedgwick collection*

Another ex-LSWR type, this time one which had started its life on express-passenger workings yet was now relegated to more mundane cross-country work: 'T6' 4-4-0 No 679 on a Bristol–Portsmouth service. Built in November 1895, it remained in service until April 1937; the last of this class of 10 engines survived until April 1943. *O. J. Morris*

Favourite amongst many devotees of Southern steam were the 'T9' class. No 286 is seen here on a West of England working — the type of duty for which the class was built, from 1899 onwards. No 286 would survive into BR days, not being withdrawn until April 1951. *Ian Allan Library*

A 'T14' at rest. Taking water, No 446 is seen in modified form after rebuilding by Drummond's successor, Robert Urie, whose preference for clamps on the lower half of the smokebox is again apparent. The continuous splasher was pierced by a single inspection door, and was of such large dimensions that the engines were nicknamed 'Paddleboxes'.
Ian Allan Library

An unusual view of an unusual design — Drummond 'T14' No 447 — at Waterloo in the summer of 1947. Visible is the reversing linkage and water feed to the clack valve from the injector. As well as the fitting of a Urie boiler the huge splashers were removed and the footplate raised to give better access.
C. C. B. Herbert

A 'Paddlebox' at work. Limited to secondary and relief workings, the 'T14s' were Urie rebuilds of Drummond 4-6-0s, and, despite having larger boilers, were never the equal of the smaller 'T9s'. No 443 is depicted near Battledown, west of Basingstoke, on a down Southampton service in August 1947. *R. E. Vincent*

Left:
Working hard on the electrified four-track section east of Brookwood, 'Paddlebox' No 460 heads a special in Southern days. One can almost imagine the harassed shed foreman having to use the engine for such a duty at peak times. *S. C. Townroe*

Below:
The Southern also inherited a number of large tank engines from the LSWR, No 492 being one of four Class G16 4-8-0s built in 1921 specifically for shunting the new hump yard at Feltham. All lasted into BR days, although regrettably none escaped scrapping. *Ian Allan Library*

Left:
Havant station in February 1937, prior to rebuilding with four through tracks. 'L12' No 421 has charge of the 3.00pm Portsmouth–Victoria. *G. J. Jefferson*

Right:
Empty stock, including Pullman coaches from a previous Ocean Liner working, heads north through Eastleigh behind 'S15' No 511. The railway scene today is little altered in so far as there are still four lines through the station, although (as might be expected) there has been rationalisation in other respects. Outside the boundary fence, offices (rather than houses) overlook the scene. *Ian Allan Library*

No 745 *Tintagel*, one of the Urie-designed batch of 'King Arthurs' (perhaps more accurately described as Class N15), stands at Waterloo prior to departure on what is clearly a test of some description, judging from the indicator shelter added to the front. This would accommodate at least two members of the test section, comfort coming a poor second to the need to obtain information on steaming, smokebox vacuum and other criteria over a particular route. *Tony Sedgwick collection*

Another Urie 'Arthur', No 748 *Iseult*, and, alongside, a superb wall of coal. Such coal stacks were built with all the skill of that necessary to form a dry stone wall and were intended to serve as emergency supplies in the event of shortage. Those responsible for such a feat were invariably the cleaners and shed labourers, whilst the coal itself would also have to be used and then replaced at intervals to prevent it 'going off' and so becoming of little use in raising steam. Again, local labour would be used for the task. *Ian Allan Library*

Running as an experimental oil-burner in October 1946, Urie-built 'King Arthur' No 740 *Merlin* is seen near Winchfield on a down Bournemouth service in October 1946. Two of the class were so converted around this time; although reasonably successful, the engines were not popular with crews — due not least to the smell and difficulties in re-lighting the oil when required — and reverted to coal-firing shortly afterwards. *M. W. Earley*

After Drummond, the locomotive policy of the LSWR was dominated by big two-cylinder designs, ironically the same policy as would be followed in the final years of BR steam. Posed for the press at Waterloo is Urie 'Arthur' No 453 *King Arthur*, displaying a pedigree not dissimilar to the Adams design of the past. *Ian Allan Library*

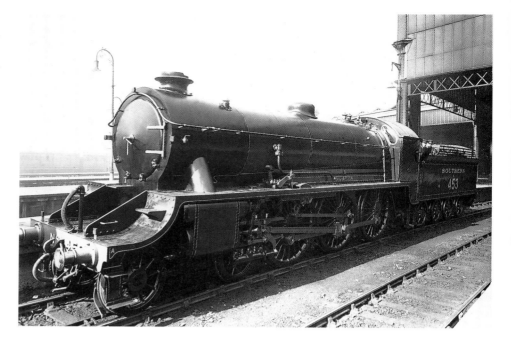

Maunsell locomotives

No E450 *Sir Kay* awaits departure from Seaton Junction in August 1930. The tender is a Drummond 'watercart' design, with the brake detail clearly displayed. The detailing of the LSWR signals is also well worth a second look. *M. T. Jenkyn*

Above:
The 'N15' class, first introduced by the LSWR and perpetuated in modified form by the SR, were popular with both crews and shed foremen. Simple, reliable machines with everything easily accessible, they would perform well on all but the fastest workings and indeed were preferred by some to the vagaries in behaviour associated with the original Bulleid Pacifics. Seen here is No 790 *Sir Villiars*, working an up special off the Bournemouth line somewhere between Basingstoke and Brookwood. *R. F. Dearden*

Centre right:
Another Brighton-line working with Pullman vehicles included in the rake: a superbly clean No E797 *Sir Blamor de Ganis*, named after perhaps one of the more obscure knights from Arthurian legend. *E. R. Wethersett*

Lower right:
Sister (or should it be brother?) engine No 803 *Sir Harry le Fise Lake* with a six-coach rake on Brighton-line duties, probably not long after the engine was built in 1927. Richard Maunsell, the first Southern CME, was clearly so impressed with this class, inherited from his predecessor on the LSWR, that he had a new batch constructed during the early 1920s, all of which survived well into BR days. These SR-built versions were fitted with modified cabs, whilst a number also had six-wheel tenders (as here) and were thus ideal for work on the shorter runs over former LBSCR lines. *E. R. Wethersett*

Arguably the best of the large tank-engine designs was Maunsell's three-cylinder 'W' class, introduced in 1932. This displayed considerable similarity to his various 2-6-0 designs, and, indeed, a number of common parts were used. Intended for cross-London freight traffic, No 1912 is depicted at Battersea in 1932 pending one such duty. More than capable of passenger work, they were never employed, being banned from doing so, although they did handle empty coaching stock. The Southern's reluctance to use tank engines on fast workings stemmed from the Sevenoaks tragedy of 1927. *E. R. Wethersett*

Of the Maunsell 2-6-0s a small number were built as three-cylinder machines and could be readily identified by the high step above the buffer-beam. No A892 awaits departure from Waterloo in the 1920s. All the Moguls were later fitted with smoke-deflectors, which altered their appearance considerably. *Ian Allan Library*

Sporting lined livery which includes the sides of the running plate, 'U' class No A638 stands at London Bridge low level. The man in the background is standing not on the cab of the locomotive but on a ledge on the wall behind. *Ian Allan Library*

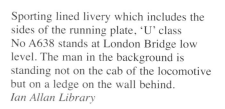

Fitted with smoke-deflectors, two-cylinder Class N Mogul No 1827 passes through Ashford, Kent, on a wartime goods working, possibly in 1941. *Southern Railway*

Stewarts Lane and green-liveried 'N' class No 1407, by now fitted with deflectors which are also in green livery. The engine is in pristine external condition, at a time when cleaning was still regarded as an essential part of locomotive preparation. *Ian Allan Library*

The first of Maunsell's 'Lord Nelson' 4-6-0s being prepared for duty at Eastleigh, in a publicity photograph released in the mid-1920s. For many years the largest steam engines on the Southern, the 16 members of this class were employed on the principal services on both Eastern and Western sections until ousted by Bulleid Pacifics. *Ian Allan Library*

Class N15 'Lord Nelson' No 30855 *Robert Blake* stands alongside the Eastleigh coaling stage in the 1950s. Of the 16 members of the class, one survived for preservation as part of the National Collection and may one day be seen back at work on former Southern lines. *Ian Allan Library*

No selection of Southern locomotives would be complete without a view of the 'Schools' or 'V' class. Arguably the best 4-4-0s of any railway, they achieved feats of haulage way beyond what would normally be expected from what was really only a medium-sized locomotive. Here No 30924 *Haileybury* is seen near Folkestone in early BR days (albeit with evidence of its previous ownership still on the tender), coupled to a mixed rake of stock including a three-coach Bulleid set. *E. R. Wethersett*

A temporary adornment was this style of fleet identification, seen applied to the tender of 'Schools' class 4-4-0 No 30926 *Repton*. Fortunately this was short-lived. *Southern Railway*

Bulleid locomotives

Certainly one of the strangest designs ever seen on Britain's railways was Bulleid's 'Q1' class, introduced in 1942 as an austerity freight engine. No C18 is pictured here in July 1942 on trial on a heavy freight; as it is wartime the location is recorded as 'Somewhere on the Southern', although in reality the location is believed to be near to Feltham. Despite their ungainly appearance, these engines were generally popular with the crews, although their braking ability was sometimes suspect when at the head of an unfitted freight. *Southern Railway*

Detail view of the rear end of a member of the 'Q1' class, showing the considerable use made of fabrication and welding techniques. The two hoses were for vacuum and steam heating, and indeed the class were used on passenger workings in later years. Notice also the two large brake cylinders on the tender. The white buffers were a temporary embellishment which would not long have remained clean in service. *British Railways*

'Q1' class No C10 is seen here within the depths of Guildford shed in May 1946. Well capable of the tasks expected of them, the 40 members of this class would last almost to the end of steam. *H. C. Casserley*

Pre-dating the 'Q1' class by just one year were the first of Bulleid's 'Merchant Navy' Pacifics, officially designated as mixed-traffic although in reality pure express locomotives. They were nevertheless seen on milk trains, primarily to/from the West Country, many of these services being of greater tonnage than a passenger train of comparative length. No 21C7 *Aberdeen Commonwealth* was recorded at Byfleet junction on a down working in August 1947. *E. R. Wethersett*

No 21C5 *Canadian Pacific* awaits departure from Brighton on a special working, not long after completion in 1942: the engine is in almost original condition with as yet no modifications made to the cab, exhaust or SOUTHERN plate; the underside of the bogie would likewise appear to be free from oil, grease and other workday dirt. *Ian Allan Library*

'Merchant Navy' No 21C8 *Orient Line*, but seen before being named, is depicted passing Surbiton on an up West of England working: the engine is at the head of a former LSWR 56ft 3-LAV set, with the remainder of the train apparently comprising Maunsell corridor coaches. All members of the class were named after shipping lines that berthed at the various Southern-owned docks and ports. *Tony Sedgwick collection*

The locomotive exchanges of 1948 have been well documented elsewhere, but it is always pleasing to come up with a 'new' photograph that has not received a wide exposure. This example shows 'Merchant Navy' No 35017 *Belgian Marine*, temporarily attached to an LMS tender and with the former LNER dynamometer car behind, climbing Holloway Bank, north of King's Cross, with the 1.10pm to Leeds on 27 May 1948. *E. R. Wethersett*

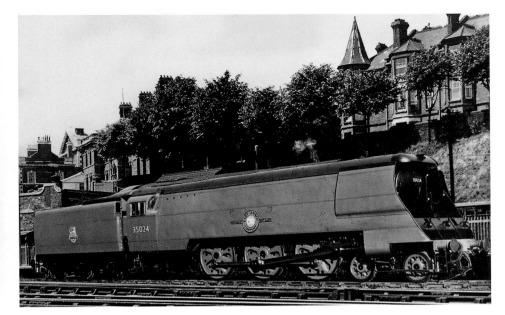

No 35024 *East Asiatic Company* stands at Exeter Central *c*1950 — when policies for locomotive design and liveries to be carried were still under consideration — in the short-lived blue colour scheme. The blue was extended to the wheel centres, and, whilst it looked smart when clean and newly applied, the labour costs of maintaining it thus led to its being superseded by Brunswick green. *W. J. Reynolds*

One of the most famous of Bulleid's 'Battle of Britain' Pacifics, No 21C151 *Winston Churchill*, depicted in almost original condition. As BR No 34051 it survived long enough in service to haul its namesake's funeral train in January 1965 and was subsequently saved for the National Collection, albeit regrettably as a static exhibit. *Ian Allan Library*

'Battle of Britain' Pacific No 21C163 (later No 34063 *229 Squadron*) at work on a South Eastern-section service, the 11.35am Victoria to Ramsgate. The engine appears to be in as-built condition, with original-style cab and wraparound fairing ahead of the cylinders. *Ian Allan Library*

Bulleid was of course principally a steam man, although he did venture into the realms of both electric and diesel traction. In the latter field the results were Nos 10201-3, which, prior to their appearance, afforded the Southern's publicity department the opportunity to exercise a degree of artistic licence. *Southern Railway*

Diesel and Electric Locomotives

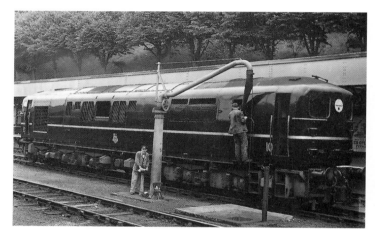

The second of the SR-ordered diesel-electric locomotives, No 10202, seen at Exeter. The engine is taking on water to replenish the oil-fired train-heating boiler. None of the boilers fitted to early diesels was particularly satisfactory; operating the equipment was the responsibility of the fireman, but on occasion he would come back with singed eyebrows and the passengers would be treated to a cold ride. *W. M. J. Jackson*

Externally similar but with an engine uprated to 2,000hp, No 10203 is seen on test with the Swindon dynamometer car near Andover in 1955. The SR diesel engines had bodywork designed by Bulleid to match the profile of his coaches. Although they were a success, the technology available at the time meant the machines displayed a low power:weight ratio, although the same could also be said of the first-generation diesels ordered by BR under the 1955 Modernisation Plan. All three survived until the 1960s, when their non-standard design rendered them obsolete. Sadly none was preserved. *G. Wheeler*

No 10203 again, but this time near the opposite end of the SR, at Tunbridge Wells West in 1954. It is likely that this was a trial working, as the engine was almost brand new and displaying the then standard livery for diesel locomotives of black and silver. Later all three engines would be repainted in standard BR Brunswick green. *A. T. H. Tayler*

Away from its original haunts, No 10201 passes Knighton Junction with a Derby–St Pancras working. All three of the SR diesels spent their later years away from the Southern and, as intended, put in much reliable work on express services, albeit for the LMR. *A. F. Taylor*

To its fleet of electric units the Southern added three main-line electric locomotives, intended primarily for goods and parcels workings. No CC2, seen at Bognor Regis with what can hardly have been a demanding load, would later become No 20002.
T. L. Smith/Tony Sedgwick collection

For a short time in the early 1950s the Southern's fleet of steam locomotives was supplemented by the two LMS-built diesel-electric locomotives, which worked turn and turn about with the Pacifics. Near Wareham on 5 September 1953, No 10000 is piloted by 'U' class 2-6-0 No 31632 on the 11am Weymouth–Waterloo. The Mogul had previously worked a stopping train from Weymouth to Wareham and was returning to Bournemouth to take up its next duty. *B. Knowlman*

EMUs

A London Bridge–Victoria working formed of set No 1805, which started life as the driving cars from an LBSCR AC overhead South London unit. It was given a major rebuild for d.c. operation and Metropolitan-Vickers supplied the electrical equipment. The flattened roof gives away the original position of the overhead bow collector. *Stephenson Locomotive Society*

2-NOL set No 1827, forming part of a train from Waterloo to Reading via Richmond. In practice, few passengers bound for Reading would use this service, most preferring the much quicker route from Paddington, which could save over an hour on the journey. *J. H. Aston*

Dating from LSWR days, three-coach set No 1679 was formed in 1928 for that year's electrification scheme. The set comprised an eight-compartment Motor Third, a Trailer Composite and a Motor Composite. Officially known as the '1201' class, they remained in service throughout World War 2 but were augmented to 4-car by 1949. *Ian Allan Library*

Another rebuild involved the three-coach sets numbered 1401-95, No 1491 being seen here. On these the bodywork was converted from ex-SECR six- and four-wheeled coaches; the finished sets were used on the Eastern section following its electrification in 1925/6. *Ian Allan Library*

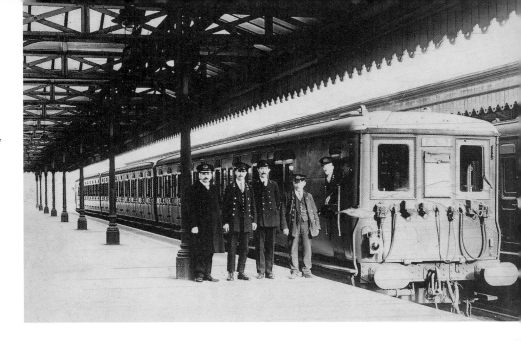

The 4-LAV units dating from 1931/2 were built at Eastleigh for use on semi-fast and slow services from Victoria to Brighton and Worthing. They performed this role for upwards of 35 years but were eventually replaced by the mass influx of 'VEP' sets in the late 1960s. Units 2922 and 2937 are depicted at Ford on the coast line, 9 July 1968. *J. Scrace*

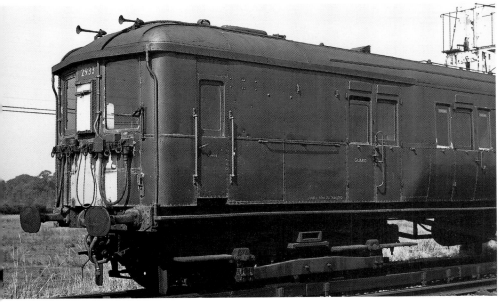

Another 4-LAV unit, No 2933, at Ford in 1968. The make-up of these units was: Motor Brake Second, Trailer Composite, Trailer Composite (Lavatory), Motor Brake Second. Notice the small yellow warning panel on what was still a green-painted unit. *J. Scrace*

There can be little doubt that the SR electric fleet was portrayed to best advantage when in green livery. With Motor Brake Second leading, '4-LAV' set No 2928 makes ready to leave Brighton for Victoria on 28 October 1968, by which time there were only four such units remaining in active service. *John Vaughan*

First-class compartment of a brand-new 4-LAV unit for the Three Bridges electrification scheme, which commenced services on Sunday 17 July 1932. Initially an hourly service was provided from both Victoria and London Bridge, enhanced at peak times. The electric service was extended to Brighton from 30 December 1932, although trial trains had been running since 2 November. *Ian Allan Library*

The Southern was in many ways a victim of its own success with electrification, as overcrowding quickly became a problem. The situation was addressed by Bulleid with the introduction of the 4-SUB units, which could take nearly 500 passengers in a four-coach set. However, the bland appearance (compared with the previous view) is apparent, and, whilst the number of passengers carried may have been high, comfort and space were clearly not a priority. *John Topham*

Above:
The LBSCR used numerical headcodes to identify its electric
services, and in SR days the practice became general, using either
letters or numbers as electrification spread across the network.
This is 4-SUB No 4324 awaiting departure on 15 August 1956
with a London Bridge to London Bridge service via Tulse Hill,
Crystal Palace and Sydenham. *J. H. Aston*

Above:
Fondly remembered still are the 4-COR sets, which spent their
lives on the Waterloo–Portsmouth services. Nicknamed 'Nelsons'
due to the headcode number that appeared in the window opposite
the driver, thus giving the ends a distinctly one-eyed appearance,
they were popular with crews and passengers alike, although in
summer months drivers would sometimes complain about the
temperature within the driving compartment. Motor coach
No 11201, seen at Preston Park Works, Brighton, at the end of its
working life, is now privately preserved. *David Brown*

Below:
Electrification to Horsham in 1937 had aroused fears from a
number of landowners and farmers in West Sussex over the danger
from the live conductor rail — so much so that questions were
asked in Parliament and suggestions made about enclosing the live
rail and having current passing through it only when a train was
imminent. None of these was sufficient to prevent progress,
however, as demonstrated by No 4233 on the 5.13pm Victoria-
Coulsdon North working at Clapham Junction on 12 May 1949.
J. H. Aston

Lined Southern Railway livery on a brand-new Third-class steel motor coach built by Metropolitan-Cammell in 1935. Even the timber beam on which the collection shoe was mounted was polished. *Ian Allan Library*

Recorded on the Quarry line in 1953, '5-BEL' set 3052 runs in tandem with another Pullman unit making the standard 10-coach train. Each set was self-contained, with restaurant and Pullman First- and Second-class seating, there being no corridor connections between the units. *Ian Allan Library*

The rather antiquated (by modern standards) driving-cab interior of 4-COR unit No 3142. It is not certain if the sun visor was an original fitting. The three gauges displayed the current drawn (in amps), speed and air pressure; the scraper on the seat was not a standard fitting! *Chris Wilson*

Another Bulleid innovation was the double-deck unit, introduced in 1949. Intended to ease overcrowding on routes where extra coaches could not be added to existing services and line capacity did not permit additional services, this represented a bold attempt at addressing a major problem. Two four-coach sets were built, which together could accommodate no fewer than 1,104 seated passengers. These photographs depict the inaugural run of the double-deck sets from Charing Cross on 2 November 1949 and show well the maximum space taken for passenger use. Not often realised is that non-standard small wheels were a necessity on these units.

Regrettably, innovation was not rewarded by success, and the design was not perpetuated. The additional time needed to load and unload passengers, allied to complaints of the cramped conditions, did little to pacify passengers or operators, and there was also at least one serious assault on a passenger hemmed in within an upper compartment. Moreover, construction of the stock to the limits of the loading gauge meant that its sphere of operation was severely restricted. Ironically, in these days of privatisation at least one rail operator is again considering double-deck trains as a means to ease overcrowding! *(both) F. G. Reynolds*

Carriage stock

Posed, no doubt, but a view of an SECR Compartment Third, complete with oil lighting. *Ian Allan Library*

Ryde Esplanade, December 1966.
The gentleman on the left bears a startling resemblance to the late Alfred Hitchcock. *Rod Hoyle*

The fear of global conflict which existed throughout the Cold War period resulted in the railways' being charged with providing mobile Civil Defence Schools. One such vehicle is seen here in the form of an ex-SECR 'birdcage' brake in October 1956. *Ian Allan Library*

Apparently in storage, ex-LSWR 57ft x 8ft 6in brake No 3162 was recorded by the camera in October 1949. *A. C. Roberts / Tony Sedgwick collection*

Staff were often given training and general information by means of the Southern's Cinema Coach, which would travel around the system and be stabled at suitable locations. On this occasion, in 1940, it was depicted at Bricklayers Arms, and, although the subject of the presentation is not recorded, it could well have been a morale-boosting exercise. Interestingly, none of the men present appears to be carrying a tin hat. *Ian Allan Library*

The 'Devon Belle' was the Southern's all-Pullman train to the west and it was provided with an observation car at the tail end. Here it is near Basingstoke in BR days in June 1950. The car was later transferred to Scotland for use on the scenic West Highland line and it was later preserved on the Paignton & Dartmouth Railway where it can be seen to this day. *Southern Railway*

Used for loading-gauge checks on bridges, tunnels and other overhead structures, this former 'birdcage' brake is seen behind 'C2X' No 32546 at Cheam. Despite the presence of the electric unit in normal service at what is obviously a relatively busy location, none of the men appears concerned about possible other traffic, whilst likewise there is not a single high-visibility jacket to be seen. *Tony Sedgwick collection*

A slightly earlier variant of the vehicle seen above and possibly of SECR design, although neither date nor location are recorded. The elongated buffers suggest the coach had been modified to deal with the sharpest of curves. *Ian Allan Library*

The standard Southern four-wheeled utility van as modified in 1944. Previously this type of vehicle had been constructed with plank bodywork; this later variant has reinforced plastic sheets instead. Even so, it was the original type that would last the longest, and numerous examples would outlive steam, until the traffic for which they had been intended also disappeared. *Ian Allan Library*

Wagon stock and miscellaneous vehicles

Milk from the West Country being unloaded at Vauxhall, at a time when most milk for the capital was transported by rail. The Southern did not, of course, have a monopoly of this type of traffic, although the farming areas west of Salisbury made it an important source of revenue. Note that the vehicles are six-wheeled — partly to spread the load but also to reduce 'hunting', which could occur at speed with short-wheelbase vehicles, the effect being to churn the milk and (if the cream content were high) turn it to butter by the time it reached its destination. *P. Ransome-Wallis*

An SR ballast-plough brake van built by
Charles Roberts of Wakefield and seen here
in the official works photograph of 1932.
The ploughs underneath could be raised or
lowered as required and was capable of
working in either direction.
Ian Allan Library

The earlier LSWR variant, capable of
working in only one direction.
Not surprisingly, these vehicles were used
almost exclusively with trains of ballast
hoppers, although no vehicle fitted with a
plough could be used for its intended
purpose on routes where there were
conductor rails, and with the general
expansion of the electrified network came a
corresponding decrease in the use of ballast
ploughs. *Stephenson Locomotive Society*

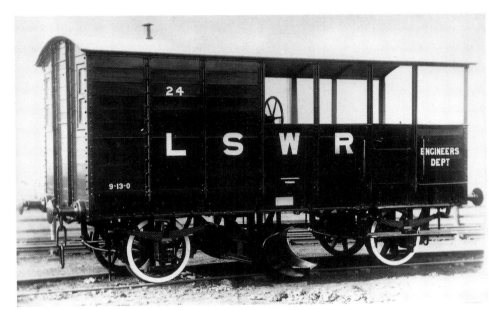

The standard SR 25-ton brake van, this
particular example — No 55964 — being
built at Lancing. Fitted only with standard
three-link couplings, it would have given
the guard a rough ride on occasion,
although the enclosed cabin would have
been warm and snug in winter.
Ian Allan Library

Another rarely photographed vehicle was this self-propelled four-wheeled Engineer's inspection trolley, No 346S, seen on the down fast line at Eastleigh. Such vehicles were used for officers' inspections within a local area and were often a hotch-potch of various components. Even so, it would have to be signalled as a train for safety. Aside from the noise from what was probably a petrol engine, the riding qualities of such a machine at anything above a crawl probably left something to be desired. *Ian Allan Library*

The Lancing Works shunter in later years was this four-wheeled petrol-engined machine. Numbered 499 in the Plant & Machinery series, it was very much a local product and owed its origins to a variety of sources; from the front it resembles a brake van and from the side a locomotive. Built in the mid-thirties, it disappeared on the closure of Lancing Works in 1963. The very short wheelbase probably allowed it to use the various 'wagon'-type turntables on the site, one of which is partially visible in the foreground. *J. H. Aston*

No 481 *Inspector*, seen here as a 2-4-2T but which started life as a 2-4-0T built by Sharp Stewart in 1869. Twenty years later, in 1889, the then LBSCR Locomotive Superintendent, William Stroudley, instructed that the engine be taken into the works at Brighton for conversion to the form seen here. Sadly he died before the work was finished, and the completed machine was therefore probably never given the amount of use that had been intended. Instead it was recorded as used primarily by the Civil Engineer and accrued just under 9,000 miles' running in six years in its new guise. It was scrapped in 1899. *Stephenson Locomotive Society*

Another unusual machine, this time muscle-powered: the Ryde (Isle of Wight) hand shunter, known affectionately as 'Midget'. Fortunately livery details of this rare vehicle have survived, indicating that it had a standard SR-brown body and black hand wheels and rail wheels; buffer-beams, side rods and nameplates were red. *Ian Allan Library*

A minor job for the Eastleigh breakdown gang, near Itchen Abbas on the Mid-Hants line one Sunday morning early in 1955. The engine, an 'M7' 0-4-4T, had broken a tyre whilst working the branch train. As the route was single-track, the crane had to approach end-on in order to lift the front end so that the remains of the tyre could be removed, after which the machine was towed slowly back to Eastleigh for repair, albeit on a somewhat uneven keel. As Stephen Townroe, then in charge at Eastleigh, put it, '… we could then all go home for some lunch'. *S. C. Townroe*

Mishaps

No 34057 *Biggin Hill* at Hamble, on the coastal line between Fareham and Southampton, on 22 May 1961, having succumbed to a rather severe casing fire. The original Pacific design was prone to this occurrence, usually caused by hot cinders or slivers from brake blocks catching oil-soaked lagging under the casing. On this occasion the services of the local fire brigade were called for and the train was declared a total failure; the engine subsequently 'skidded' into a nearby private siding, where fitters from Eastleigh removed the brake rigging in order to tow it to Eastleigh for repair. Passing on the opposite line is the 8.10am from Bristol behind an unidentified Standard Class 4. *P. Fagan / Tony Sedgwick collection*

The Haywards Heath accident of 14 November 1925 which involved Atlantic No B421. The engine was at the head of the 9.40am West Worthing–London express when the rear coupled axle fractured. Fortunately the train was not derailed and there were no injuries, although there were considerable delays to subsequent traffic. The engine is seen here with its tender already removed and with what is believed to be the Brighton breakdown crane in attendance.
Tony Sedgwick collection

The effects of enemy action at Nine Elms, 1 October 1940. Among the casualties is 'T14' No 458, which (not surprisingly, perhaps) was considered beyond economic repair. *Tony Sedgwick collection*

'Minor' damage to 'K' class 2-6-0 No 32347, seen here at Bricklayers Arms after a confrontation with 'D' class 4-4-0 No 31741 at Rotherhithe Road on 14 October 1951. Both engines were subsequently repaired, No 32347 remaining in service until the end of 1962.
Tony Sedgwick collection

Aftermath of the accident at Vauxhall on 29 August 1912. The engine, a 'T9' 4-4-0, was running tender-first from Nine Elms to Waterloo, to work a boat train. Unfortunately the driver misread the signals approaching the station and collided at some speed with the rear of the 6.37am from Aldershot, which was stationary at Vauxhall while tickets were being collected. One passenger died, and 52 people (including two railway staff) were injured. Of the coaches visible, the Brake Third is No 1519, whilst the Composite can be identified as No 385, forming part of set No 63. The Nine Elms breakdown crane is in attendance. *(all) Ian Allan Library*

Works

Part of the former LBSCR carriage works at Lancing, west of Brighton, the site of which is now an industrial estate. Here the designs of Billinton, Marsh and the like were turned from drawings into reality. Following nationalisation, carriage building was concentrated at Eastleigh, and today there is nothing (save the shells of a few buildings) to indicate its former use.
Ian Allan Library

Preceding the works at Eastleigh, which later became the principal locomotive works for the whole of the Southern Railway, was that at Nine Elms (London). The photograph is dated 1908, but may have been some few years earlier.
Tony Sedgwick

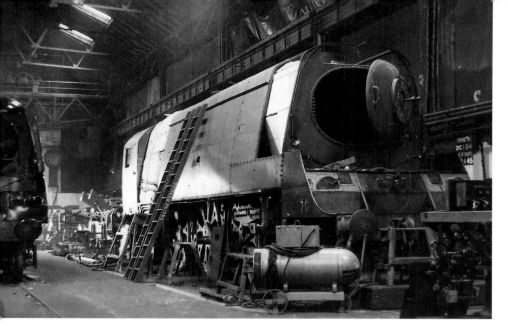

Brighton Works in 1945, with two members of the lighter 'West Country' class under construction. The locomotive on the left is No 21C102 *Salisbury*; that on the right, as yet incomplete, would become No 21C104 *Yeovil*.
Ian Allan Library

Inside the works at Eastleigh, 'Schools' class No 30901 *Winchester* reposes temporarily as an 0-2-0 during the course of a heavy overhaul. As the motion is connected and the driving wheel is sitting on rollers it is possible that valve setting was taking place. The locomotive is understandably supported by jacks and packing — necessary not only to keep the machine on an even keel but also to ensure excessive strain was not placed upon the springs and axleboxes.
Stephenson Locomotive Society

Class A1X 'Terrier' 0-6-0T No 32635 seen at Brighton towards the end of its days as Works shunter in June 1961, by which time its Stroudley 'improved engine green' (yellow) livery was beginning to show signs of wear. It would survive until March 1963. *J. C. Haydon*

The original steam crane from Nine Elms, numbered here as Loco Department No 1. Like locomotives, cranes were moved around the system to suit changing traffic patterns, this particular example, built in 1906 by Stothert & Pitt of Bath, later being transferred to Eastleigh. *Tony Sedgwick collection*

Cranes

Left:
Overkill? There is no clue as to whether the crane driver is carrying his own means of transport or whether the cycle was simply in the way of the crane and has had to be lifted clear of the track. In this scene, recorded at Dover in the late 1950s, the majority of the public are seemingly more interested in the crane rather than its somewhat unusual load. *Kent Messenger*

Right:
How the mighty have fallen: former Brighton Atlantic No 32425 *Trevose Head* in use as a stationary boiler at Slade Green. It was on such engines that many a new fireman would learn the rudiments of his trade. *Stephenson Locomotive Society*

The depot at Hither Green, intended primarily for servicing steam locomotives working the various freight yards, was opened by the Southern in 1933; there were six dead-end roads as well as a turntable and coaling stage — both out of camera to the right. This undated BR-era view includes a selection of Moguls, at least one 'W' class 2-6-4T and a couple of 'C' class engines, together with a diesel shunter. The trackwork on at least one of the shed roads appears not to have received attention for some time. *N. E. W. Skinner*

Sheds

The interior of the repair shops at Bricklayers Arms, the principal shed of the former SECR in the London area. Developed over the years in piecemeal fashion, it survived until 1962, by which time steam had ceased working out of Charing Cross and Canon Street. In this 1958 view an unidentified 'C' class 0-6-0 and a 'Battle of Britain' Pacific — No 34087 *145 Squadron* — are under repair. *Stephenson Locomotive Society*

Ashford depot in May 1948, with 'C' class No 31695 still displaying its SR number (1695). Ashford was also the location of the SECR's main works, which would continue to be utilised for major maintenance following the end of steam. *J. H. Aston*

Norwood Junction shed, dating from 1935, was a five-road depot similar in many respects to that at Hither Green. Again, its main purpose was to service steam locomotives use on freight work around the London area, although its use declined from early BR days with the influx of diesel shunters, which required less depot servicing. It would nevertheless survive as a steam shed until 1964, in its final years taking over some of the allocation from the former steam sheds at Bricklayers Arms and Stewarts Lane. *Stephenson Locomotive Society*

Brighton shed in 1960 with a survivor from the 19th century, 'E4' class 0-6-2T No 32512, which was then nearing the end of its days. The 'E4s' represented a development by Billinton of the earlier 'E3' design but with larger wheels. Later they were rebuilt by Earle Marsh with a larger boiler and smokebox, and the SR continued the alterations by reducing their cylinder diameter by ½in, to 17½in.
J. C. Baker

Upper right:
A panoramic view of Ramsgate shed in July 1939, 20 years before steam would be ousted from principal workings into Kent. No fewer than 27 steam locomotives are visible, from Classes B1, C, D, D1, E, E1, F1, H, L, L12, O1, T9, U1 and N15 ('King Arthurs' Nos 765 and 802) — proof that during Southern days, former Western-section engines did indeed venture into pastures new. *Stephenson Locomotive Society*

Below:
The former steam shed at Deal, which ceased to have an allocation of steam prior to 1923. It is recorded here from a passing train in May 1959, apparently whilst in use for wagon storage. Despite the many years without an allocation, the turntable is still extant. *Ian Allan Library*

Lower right:
The former SECR shed at Reading, recorded on 6 June 1937. The original caption states that 14 engines were present (from Classes F1, L11, R, R1 and U), three of which were in the shed and are thus not visible. Behind the shed, at a higher level, is the GWR main line, with Reading East main signalbox slightly further on. *Stephenson Locomotive Society*

The LBSCR depot in the London area, at New Cross Gate, was opened in 1839. 'D1' class 0-4-2T No 2357 was recorded outside one of the many covered areas of the shed — possibly alongside the 'Octagon' roundhouse — in March 1939. The depot would remain operational until 1951 and survive in derelict condition for some years thereafter. *E. R. Wethersett*

Eastbourne shed is seen here in June 1950. At least four engines are identifiable, the line on the right being headed by 'E4' 0-6-2Ts Nos 32575 and 32405 and 'H1' Atlantic No 32038 *Portland Bill*; on the left is 'D3' 0-4-4T No 32368. *E. R. Wethersett*

Newhaven, on the Sussex coast, in July 1926, with a quantity of tank engines awaiting disposal. According to the record the locomotives involved were Nos A366, A50, A58, A423, A363, A413, A403 and A415, all members of Stirling's 'Q' class which had been rebuilt by Wainwright as Class Q1, and had been displaced by South Eastern suburban electrification. *H. C. Casserley / Tony Sedgwick collection*

Strawberry Hill depot in 1920, with a number of Robinson-designed former ROD 2-8-0s stored pending disposal; the LSWR used a few of the class on a temporary basis, but these were never taken into actual stock. Known initially as Fulwell Junction depot, Strawberry Hill had opened in 1897, replacing a number of smaller sheds in the area. It would itself be superseded with the opening of the new steam shed at Feltham by 1924 although the site remained in use, albeit stripped of its former steam facilities, for stabling electric units. *Tony Sedgwick*

Feltham depot in October 1965, with 'N' class No 31873 (unofficially adorned with the reversed version of the then-new BR symbol) and, behind it, BR Standard Class 3 2-6-2T No 82023. The depot illustrates the Southern's propensity for using concrete whenever possible. *J. Scrace*

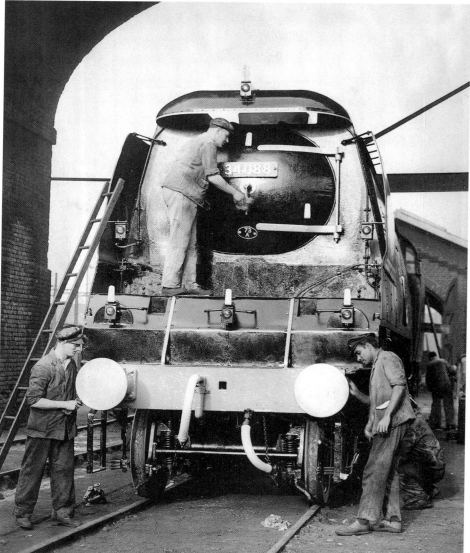

The state visit of the Emperor of Abyssinia and his son to London in October 1954 resulted in a special steam-hauled working from Portsmouth. The engine selected, No 34088 *213 Squadron*, is seen here receiving a final polish at Stewart's Lane. Aside from the buffers — probably exchange items used solely for such workings — the vacuum and steam-heat pipes are also painted white, as are the lamp irons. Mr Bulleid would surely have approved. *Ian Allan Library*

The artistic perspective: a line of water columns at Nine Elms in the final days of steam, 1967. *Ian Allan Library*

The expansive electric depot at Wimbledon, with a number of sets awaiting duty. In the foreground '0395' No 30573 is delivering spares and cautiously reversing into the depot. To the right is the incline leading up to the power station, worked by small DC electric locomotives, one of which may just be discerned on a train of coal approaching on the right. *Ian Allan Library*

The Southern had only a handful of roundhouse sheds and Guildford, shown here, was a semi-roundhouse, the cramped conditions of the site making this a necessity. Despite its presence within an electrified network, it would maintain a steam allocation to the very end, but is seen here in 1930, with 'A12' No 554 and 'M7' No 53. *Tony Sedgwick*

Another panoramic shed scene, this time at Basingstoke on 25 April 1937. Here again, 14 engines were noted, from classes G6, H2, L12, O2, S11, S15, T6, U and X6. Of the two 'X6s' present, No 657 would soon be used on the remains of the Basingstoke & Alton line during the making of the film *Oh Mr Porter! Stephenson Locomotive Society*

An instantly recognisable location, Eastleigh, and the rear of the shed, with the stores and mess-rooms on the extreme left. The products of Adams, Drummond and Urie can be seen, although it does not appear there are any Maunsell designs present. Eastleigh was the principal depot for Southampton, although small sub-sheds survived at Southampton Terminus station and within the docks complex.
Ian Allan Library

Exmouth Junction-based 'N' class 2-6-0 No 31830 at Eastleigh in April 1960. The engine has received new frames and cylinders with outside steam pipes and a BR-style chimney, and is no doubt being prepared for a return to its home area.
C. P. Boocock

Seven miles south of Winchester was Eastleigh — mecca for the steam enthusiast. Aside from engines in regular service there would invariably be a line of locomotives out of steam, awaiting either works attention or scrapping. For this line-up, it was generally the former course of action, 'E4s' Nos 32492, 32556, 32491, 32562 and 32559 being recorded on 28 August 1954. *Tony Sedgwick*

Almost at the end of their working days, Drummond '700' class engines Nos 30316 and 30306 stand at the Eastleigh coaling stage in 1962. Built in 1897, the class was used primarily on goods services throughout their lives, the simplicity of the design meaning they were cheap to maintain and would repay their construction costs many times over. Sadly none survives in preservation. *D. Fereday Glenn*

A personal favourite of the author — rebuilt 'West Country' No 34046 *Braunton* — stabled outside Bournemouth shed. Upon the locomotives' withdrawal from Eastleigh in 1966, the smokebox numberplates from this engine and No 34085 were purchased for the (then) princely sum of 25/- (£1.25). I could have had more at similar rates, but funds were the problem. Both were sold a year later, although one would have to add a few noughts on the end for today's prices! *R. Wales*

There were two sheds in the immediate Bournemouth area — the main depot at Bournemouth Central station and a smaller one at Branksome. The Branksome site was located within the triangle of lines that also led to/from Bournemouth West and was the Southern's preferred choice for a large new depot for the whole area, although this was never built; instead the small Branksome shed served to handle the engines of some trains arriving at Bournemouth West as well as an overspill to the main shed. In addition, it serviced locomotives working to/from the Somerset & Dorset line. On 2 April 1934, however, there were just three engines visible; Eastleigh-based 'L11' class 4-4-0 No 157 is seen tender-first outside the shed, whilst inside are 'A12' 2-4-0s Nos 531 and 631. *Stephenson Locomotive Society*

The LSWR shed at Salisbury opened in 1901 and had 10 roads under cover. Serving the need for engine changing on a number of trains working to/from the West Country, the allocation consisted of a large number of main-line locomotives. Additionally the depot was responsible for local and shunting duties, and, in consequence, examples of most Southern types were at some time allocated to the shed. *Stephenson Locomotive Society*

Busy times at Salisbury on 19 August 1939, with no fewer than six locomotives coupled together, having left the nearby shed and about to be dispersed to their respective duties. This was common practice at busy locations and reduced line occupancy as well as making it easier for the signalman, who would have to set the route from the shed only once. Even so, he would have to have been told how many were in the line-up! For the record, the locomotives are 'G6' No 351, 'T9' No 713, 'S11' No 395, 'K10' No 342, 'T9' No 712 and 'S11' No 463. *G. O. P. Pearce*

Beattie '0298' class 2-4-0WT No 30587 is turned at Amesbury on 14 May 1955 after working a Railway Enthusiasts' Club special from Andover to Bulford. *J. H. Aston*

The interior of Yeovil shed in June 1926, with Drummond 'C8' class 4-4-0 No E294 underneath the sheer legs (although not apparently under repair). The 'C8' class comprised 10 engines built at Nine Elms in 1898 and lasted in service until the 1930s. No 294 would be the first to be withdrawn, in February 1933, with the last of the class going less than five years later.
H. C. Casserley / Tony Sedgwick collection

Principal amongst the sheds in the western area of the Southern was the big depot at Exmouth Junction, which was the parent depot to the sub-sheds on the former LSWR lines westwards as well as to the small depots on the various branch lines in the area. In later years it was home to a number of Bulleid Pacifics, No 35024 *East Asiatic Company* being seen in almost original condition and complete with headboard *J. H. Aston/ Stephenson Locomotive Society*

Stations

Whilst the LSWR's Waterloo may have had the greater number of platforms, the LBSCR's London Terminus at Victoria had the longest, although the SECR's Cannon Street arguably had the best architectural design. When this scene was recorded at Victoria *c*1900, the monarch of the same name was still on the throne, electrification was yet to come, and horse power, in its literal form, provided the taxi!
Ian Allan Library

Of the three principal constituents of the Southern, the LSWR was the largest player, its route mileage, locomotive stock and infrastructure almost greater than those of the LBSCR and SECR combined. This photograph of the former LSWR terminus at Waterloo, dating from May 1958, could have been taken at almost any time in the preceding three decades, while the changes that would radically alter the whole appearance of the site were still some 10 years away. How many have met — or bade farewell — under the famous clock? *Stephenson Locomotive Society*

Waterloo as it existed until rebuilt for the Channel Tunnel trains. 'Battle of Britain' No 34057 *Biggin Hill* leaves with the 5.41pm Salisbury service. Also visible are another Bulleid Pacific and a BR Standard Class 4, while sheltering under the overall roof are a 'D65xx' (Class 33) diesel and a number of electric units, including a '4-COR'. *J. Scrace*

Wimbledon, in the Capital's southwestern suburbs, with a 'Schools' class 4-4-0 nearing the end of its journey. *Bernard Alfieri*

The Southern Railway was arguably at the forefront of construction techniques in its use of concrete for its 1930s station-rebuilding programme, and a variety of ultra-modern designs ensued. One of these was at Surbiton, which survives today; in this early view *c*1938 its bold, utilitarian form makes contemporary road vehicles seem old-fashioned and out of place. *Ian Allan Library*

The modern design ethos for stations was not confined to the exterior styling, the interiors of the 1930s providing (quite literally) a stark contrast with the fuss and fancy tracery of the Victorian and Edwardian eras. This is the general waiting room at Surbiton, its hard wooden benches no doubt deterring passengers from dwelling too long. *Ian Allan Library*

Despite though the widespread use of concrete, the steam train does not seem out of place at the new Surbiton as an 'S15' 4-6-0 passes through the newly-rebuilt station shortly after completion. *R. Clark*

The rebuilt station at Woking, with 4-COR set No 3116 heading
what is probably a 12-coach formation on a Portsmouth working.
J. H. Aston

A variant on the design but retaining the modern concept was
at Chessington North, where brickwork was used instead of
concrete, producing what is perhaps a more mellow effect.
This was the exterior, recorded in the last days of peace in 1939,
the blank noticeboards yet to receive their first posters.
Ian Allan Library

The advantages of concrete were demonstrated when platform extensions or alterations were contemplated, as pre-cast sections — obtained from the SR's own concrete works at Exmouth Junction — could be fitted together and then simply incorporated as required. Hundreds of locations were dealt with in this manner, this particular instance being at St Johns in 1953. The retaining wall had received similar treatment. *Ian Allan Library*

Allhallows station, at the end of its branch from Gravesend Central, was an unusual use of concrete materials for the platform whilst retaining traditional wooden structures for the buildings. From Stoke Junction on the Port Victoria branch the 1¾ miles of new track were opened as late as 16 May 1932. Unfortunately, traffic to the new resort, opposite Southend-on-Sea, did not reach expectations and the line closed on 3 December 1961. *Ian Allan Library*

Another example of the concrete plague — pre-cast concrete platform slabs, concrete fence-posts and a concrete footbridge. Other items not illustrated included permanent way and fogman's huts, the former assembled off site and built to comply with the loading gauge so they could be easily transported to where they were required and then off-loaded by crane onto a prepared base. This view is of Southease & Rodmell, on the Lewes–Newhaven line. *J. Scrace*

At Eastleigh, spanning what was known as the Salisbury loop (or, more accurately, Platform 1) was this barrow crossing, which allowed loaded platform trolleys to be wheeled across from the parcels office to the first of the island platforms. A lift from Platforms 1 and 2 up to the covered footbridge then allowed access to a second lift leading down to Platforms 3 and 4. Such a crossing was interlocked with the signalling, the man on duty at Eastleigh West signalbox being able to permit such movements when no train was signalled into the loop. This scene was recorded on 22 July 1965. *Ian Allan Library*

Another fine example of the contemporary style was at Southampton, although here only the down side was dealt with. Sadly, bombing a few years later tore a great hole within the structure, which was never repaired entirely in keeping with the original design. Nearest the camera is the passenger area whilst beyond is that dealing with parcels. *Ian Allan Library*

For many years the LSWR's Plymouth terminus was at Devonport, where a substantial brick-and-stone building was provided. Sadly rationalisation brought about by limited revenue meant all passenger traffic was concentrated at the former GWR station of Plymouth North Road, and it is no longer possible to commence a journey to Waterloo from here and running via Tavistock and Okehampton. *Ian Allan Library*

To the west of Plymouth was Callington, terminus of the Plymouth, Devonport & South Western line from Bere Alston. At one time this line had its own steam engines — *A. S. Harris, Lord St Levan* and *Earl of Mount Edgcumbe* — all of which survived into BR ownership. *R. E. Vincent*

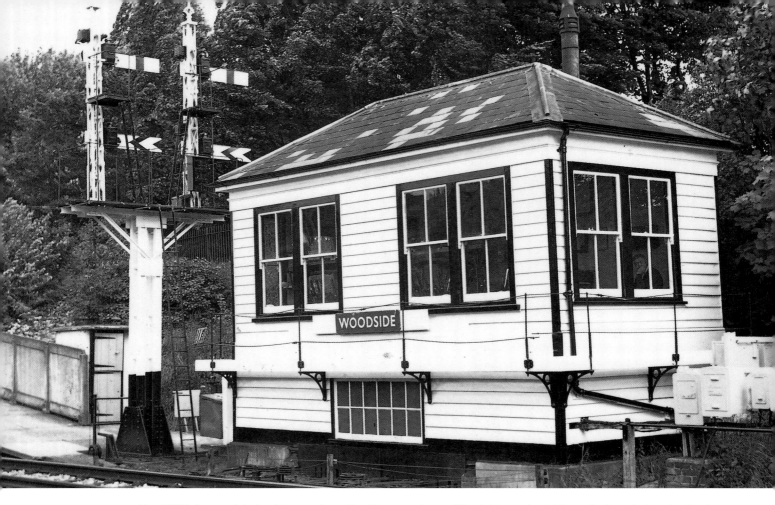

The SECR favoured timber for a number of its 'boxes, as here at Woodside, on the Addiscombe branch, junction for the link line to Sanderstead. Despite the rather bland appearance, the brackets supporting the walkway are worth a second glance. *J. Scrace*

Signalboxes

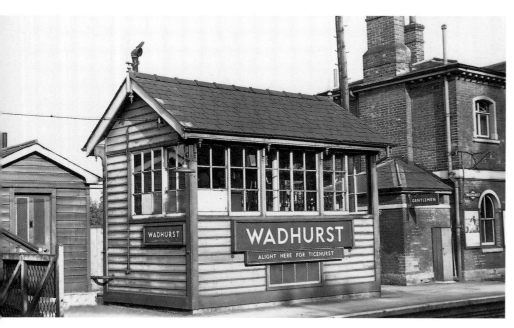

South of Tunbridge Wells were the station and signalbox at Wadhurst, recorded here in September 1969. This is probably one of the simplest of the SECR designs and lasted until control of the area was given over to Multiple Aspect Signalling. *J. Scrace*

A view of Woolwich Arsenal signalbox in its final days in 1969, showing the extension for that most important of facilities — the signalman's 'privvy'. Interestingly, the point-rodding emerges from the ends of the structure rather than conventionally from the front, although it is also visible in the foreground, on the opposite side of the running rails. *J. Scrace*

A rather diminutive structure, this time at Deal Junction. Here the 'box is supported on a brick plinth — helpful in reducing the risk of rotting of the timber — while the staircase makes a 90° turn due to the proximity of the cutting and trackwork. *J. Scrace*

The interior of the SECR's 'St Johns B Cabin' near Lewisham, complete with train-describers (the rotary instruments visible on the left and right). Those with the 'pegs' would be used by the signalman to 'describe' a train on to the next signalbox, whilst the instruments above would receive similar messages from the signalboxes nearby. In this way the signalmen would be able to identify the destination and type of each train — vital at busy locations, where several services of like formation could follow each other. *Ian Allan Library*

Signalboxes on the constituent companies
of the Southern began to appear from about
1860, with each concern favouring its own
designs. The LBSCR put its 'boxes on
stilts, the idea being to give the 'bobby' a
better view. With the technology of
signalling rapidly gaining pace, these early
'boxes were redundant within a short time;
this view shows the original structure
at Lovers' Walk, Brighton, in 1882 —
the year it was replaced by the more
modern building just visible on the left.
Stephenson Locomotive Society

Another LBSCR design, this time at
Warnham, on the line from Leatherhead to
Horsham. The LBSCR had now developed
a 'house style' with small windows above
the main sliding frames. The length of rail
bolted across the front served to keep the
brickwork in line and to act as an additional
support against which the locking frame
was anchored. *J. Scrace*

Away though from the London area, re-signalling was less of a priority; at locations such as Portsmouth, mechanical operation reigned supreme until the 1960s. This was the LBSCR-design 'box at Portsmouth Yard, complete with the typical SR green-and-white name board of later years. Not many miles away, Chichester 'box is one of the last remaining LBSCR examples, its future now fortunately secure following its inclusion as a listed structure. *British Railways*

The interior at Portsmouth, with one of the signalmen supposedly caught in the act of actually moving a lever, although, as this was an official view from the Public Relations Department. Clearly the 'posed' photograph was taken to record the scene in the final days of mechanical operation: a number of the levers have been cut down, implying electrical operation, whilst others have been taken out of use, their catch handles removed. *British Railways*

Another tall LBSCR design, but this time in the more conventional brick. At the time, every level crossing was guarded by at least a gate-box, and on busy routes these were usually signalboxes in their own right. The gates provided were ideal for protecting both the railway and road users at a time when the horse and cart ruled supreme; however, as the 'mechanical horse' began to appear and road traffic increased, they proved no match, and accordingly a number of these crossings were replaced by bridges. *Ian Allan Library*

Progress with signalling was not confined to the London area or to the 1930s; decades earlier the LSWR had instigated a pneumatic system on the main line west of Brookwood, following experiments at Grateley as early as 1902. A feature of the installation on the four-track section was the succession of gantries spanning the tracks in either direction, this one supporting the down starting signals at Farnborough. No 30746 *Pendragon* awaits departure for Basingstoke on 29 September 1951. *R. D. Swift*

Another large former LSWR 'box, this time at Northam Junction, outside Southampton. I well remember this particular location and one of the regular men, Terry Cooper. It was he who would provide me with endless cups of tea, both on late shift and at night, whilst I worked the 'box, sending (it seemed) endless trains to and from Southampton Central — all highly unofficial, of course! *J. Scrace*

A much smaller LSWR structure, albeit still displaying its origins, at Wareham in Dorset. For many years the signalman here had a level crossing to control as well, but this was later replaced by a bridge, no doubt to sighs of relief from both motorists and signalman. The gaps in the brickwork allowed the wires and rodding to emerge and also explained why signalboxes could be draughty places. *J. Scrace*

The LSWR had two other principal signalbox types, one having a centre pillar between the front windows and the other being this smaller type upon which the windows were perched high up. Dean is still served by the line between Romsey and Salisbury, although the 'box is but a memory. *J. Scrace*

Nearby was this signalbox at the similarly named Dean Hill, installed to control a set of military sidings. As might be presumed from its somewhat austere appearance, it was of wartime build; such structures were often unpopular with signalmen, being particularly cold in winter. *J. Scrace*

Despite the Depression of the early 1930s, the Southern continued its process of updating infrastructure, including replacement of mechanical signalling at Waterloo with a new power 'box. When this scene was recorded, on a wet March day in 1936, the old installation had just 6½ months left before being swept away as part of the Waterloo–Hampton Court re-signalling project. The new Waterloo power 'box then introduced would survive until the major rebuilding of the station in the late 1980s to accommodate Channel Tunnel traffic. *Ian Allan Library*

Old and new at Waterloo late in 1936. The new power 'box is located to the left and had just been commissioned, whilst spanning the tracks is a conglomeration of mechanical 'boxes which, together with their supporting bridgework, would soon be consigned to history. *Ian Allan Library*

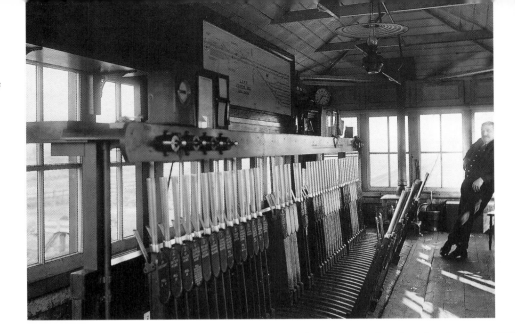

Another signalbox interior, this time at Feltham East. Here the signalman controlled the eastern entry and exit to the massive 'hump' yard, once the starting point or destination of so many of the Southern's freight services, yet nowadays utterly devoid of track *Ian Allan Library*

An example of the Southern 'greenhouse'-type 'boxes of the 1930s, this one being at Strood Junction, although there were similar structures at numerous other locations, including Woking, Templecombe and Bognor Regis, to name but three. Aside from the latest in mechanical signalling, the design incorporated a sizeable relay room on the lower floor. The first signs of Health & Safety awareness are apparent in the form of barriers opposite the access doors and wooden protection to the conductor rails where needed. *E. R. Wethersett*

The interior of Strood Junction, recorded on 17 June 1939. In locations such as this, mechanical working, allied to some electrical operation, had almost reached its zenith, as the next stage would be route setting, with a change from the conventional semaphore. Notice in particular the two detonator-placing levers, identified by black/white horizontal banding. *E. R. Wethersett*

Signalbox construction — not demolition! This is the new 'box being erected at Grove Park in late 1938, the lever frame having been pre-assembled at Wimbledon Signal Works. Clearly this represented an interim stage pending full electric operation, as, although a mechanical system is being installed, the number of short levers indicates almost half of the operation will be through electric motors.
Ian Allan Library

Contemporaneous with the construction of modern station buildings was that of similarly-styled signalboxes, one of which — at Horsham — is seen here to advantage when new in the 1930s. The lofty operating area afforded the signalman a good view of trains, whilst the lower level not only housed the mechanical and electrical interlocking but invariably also provided a base for the local S&T Department staff.
Ian Allan Library

The signalbox at Old Kew Junction was of the wartime ARP variant and consisted of stout brick outer walls with a concrete roof and thus a degree of blast protection. A number of these were erected by the Southern, although few survive today.
J. Scrace

The interior of Blackfriars Junction signalbox, with panels removed to show the various relays. This was a one-lever-one-movement operation, with mechanical interlocking between levers. *Ian Allan Library*

The interior of Borough Market Junction signalbox, for some time considered one of the busiest of all SR route 'boxes. The system worked by means of route setting, whereby the operation of one lever set the requisite route, the settings being indicated by the lights on the panel behind. Also provided were an illuminated diagram and train describers. *Ian Allan Library*

West of Salisbury, modernisation by BR in the 1950s meant that a number of the old LSWR-style 'boxes were swept away in favour of what was then the latest design, although this example at Honiton clearly has its origins in the LSWR 'centre pillar' type mentioned earlier. The lives of many of these new 'boxes would be severely curtailed due to changing traffic patterns in the 1960s, and few survive in use today. *Ian Allan Library*

Cannon Street and what is undoubtedly a special working — in fact a Derby Day Pullman special on 30 May 1951 — with 'N1' 2-6-0 No 31879 in charge. As with the 'U1' type, the three-cylinder Moguls could be identified by the raised footplating at the front. This particular example was built at Ashford in 1930 and withdrawn in November 1962. None of the 'U1' or 'N1' classes would see preservation. *J. H. Aston*

Around the South Eastern Section

Newly rebuilt 'West Country' No 34025 *Whimple* at the head of a passenger working at Cannon Street on 23 April 1958, the train being the 6.14pm to Ramsgate. By this time the days of steam working over the former SECR lines were fast drawing to a close, leading to the cascading of larger engines to the Western section and consequent scrapping of older types. *J H. Aston*

Petts Wood in July 1959. The conductor rail is in place and steam is relegated to parcels workings. The now-preserved No 30777 *Sir Lamiel* passes a group of very hot-looking maintenance men, the lack of any visible exhaust from the engine indicating the summer temperature. *Derek Cross*

No 767 *Sir Valence* with an eight-wheeled SR-design tender (note the outside axleboxes) pictured near Orpington, long before electrification of the SECR section. *Ian Allan Library*

Fruit traffic at Paddock Wood, although hardly profitable, with just one van! The fireman is no doubt scanning the horizon to see if there is any indication as to when his train will be able to leave. The Southern-design bogie brake van at the rear has the word 'reserved' on a white background. Bogie goods brake vans were unique to the SR, the first batch being built on the underframes of the former LBSCR overhead-electric motor cars. *W. A. Corkill*

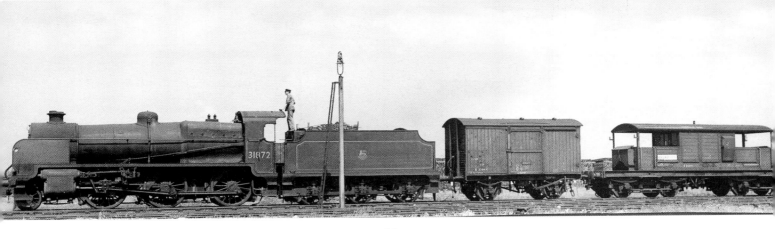

Busy times at Paddock Wood on 10 April 1952. On the left is No 31666, an 0-4-4T dating from LCDR days, on the push-pull working to Maidstone. Opposite is 1926-built 'King Arthur' class 4-6-0 No 30805 *Sir Constantine* with a Tonbridge–Ashford stopping service, while, running through on the down main line, No 34103 *Calstock* is in charge of a boat train from Victoria to Dover. *Rev A. W. V. Mace*

Upper right:
Folkestone away from the glamour of the boat trains, and the mundane but essential task of shunting, performed here by 'H' class 0-4-4T No 31328. Engines of this class had long and useful lives, this particular example being built at Ashford in December 1906 and withdrawn for scrap in February 1961. *J. H. Aston*

Lower right:
Above the streets of Folkestone this time and what could well be a boat train behind No 34076 *41 Squadron* with tender still in almost original condition. Although the photograph is undated, the engine has the early BR crest on the tender, while the then-new Mk 1 coach behind the tender implies a prestige working. *Stephenson Locomotive Society*

Another unrebuilt 'Battle of Britain' Pacific, but this time with a modified tender, with rear raves removed in an attempt to make access easier. No 34067 *Tangmere,* seen waiting signals at Faversham on 29 May 1958, was one of four of the class commemorating the names of the wartime fighter stations in Sussex and Kent. *Stephenson Locomotive Society*

No 31803, a 'U' class 2-6-0, in charge of the 4.30pm Dover–Charing Cross service on 3 August 1954. The train would appear to be made up of at least two three-coach rakes of former SECR 'birdcage' stock, so called because the guard's lookout compartment protruded above the general roof level. Note the concrete overbridge. *W. A. Corkill*

Of the four pre-nationalisation companies, the Southern probably had the largest interest in docks and shipping, thanks to considerable cross-Channel trade from Ramsgate, Dover, Folkestone and Newhaven. This is the approach to the terminus at Dover, with the top of Dover Marine station just visible in the background. Low tide reveals the less-than-neat appearance of the harbour walls. Taken in February 1944 the beach, and port, defences can be seen. *British Railways*

Double-heading of an unusual kind: 'N' class 2-6-0 No 31818 pilots 'O1' 0-6-0 No 31258 past Kearsney Junction with the 1.40pm from Shepherds' Well on 2 May 1960. Although within the haulage power of one engine, this working often had a second locomotive added to provide additional braking. *Derek Cross*

The bleak countryside that surrounded much of the Allhallows branch is typified here. 'H' class 0-4-4T No 31500 leaves Middle Stoke Halt, a pure Southern concrete specimen where the shelter was doubtless a necessity. *M. Esau*

As explained previously, the 'Q1' class 0-6-0s occasionally found themselves on passenger workings, albeit mostly branch-line work in the later days of steam. Here, however, one is shown on empty coaching stock, leaving Appledore (Kent) for Ashford on 21 February 1961. *M. Edwards*

Steam and electric: 'E6' No 32414 on a Norwood–Waddon Marsh goods crosses to the West Croydon–Wimbledon single line at West Croydon in July 1952 as 2-WIM unit No 1812 waits quietly in the background. *A. A. Sellman / Tony Sedgwick collection*

Around the Central Section

On 28 April 1928, prior to electrification of the Brighton line, 'King Arthur' class 4-6-0 No 796 *Sir Dodinas le Savage* heads a mixed rake of 12 coaches near Star Bridge, Hooley. Much of the stock appears ancient compared with the nearly new locomotive. The seventh vehicle is a Pullman coach. *E. R. Wethersett*

A truly mixed working with Class A1X 'Terrier' No B647 on what was probably a train of overhauled vehicles from Lancing Carriage Works. The coach, is an ex-LSWR 48ft Third. *Tony Sedgwick collection*

Sunday excursions would often result in through carriage workings from other Regions, as here in June 1958, with an Enfield Town–Eastbourne working south of Quarry Tunnel with 'U1' No 31891 in charge. Such duties were often the province of 'passed' men (firemen qualified to act as drivers), providing a welcome opportunity for additional experience — and often overtime. *Stanley Creer*

The steam-hauled 'Southern Belle', precursor to the 'Brighton Belle', actually pre-dated the Southern Railway, being introduced by the LBSCR in 1908. The train is seen here passing Patcham (north of Brighton) in 1922, headed by then-new Billinton 'L' class 4-6-4T No 332. *Ian Allan Library*

The 'Southern Belle' in Southern days is seen at Merstham behind Marsh Atlantic No B421. *Pamlin Prints*

Introduced into service in the early 1930s as part of a large fleet of new stock for the electrified Brighton line, the three '5-BEL' units set a world first for an electric all-Pullman service. Confined throughout their lives to the Brighton–Victoria route, they remained in service until ousted as non-standard by BR in the 1970s, and are still sorely missed by many. Set No 3053 is seen awaiting departure from Brighton on 29 May 1968. *J. Scrace*

Marsh 'J2' class 4-6-2T No 2326, formerly *Bessborough*, at work on the northbound 'Sunny South Express' near Falmer (between Lewes and Brighton) in 1936 with a train of LMS stock. *C. C. B. Herbert*

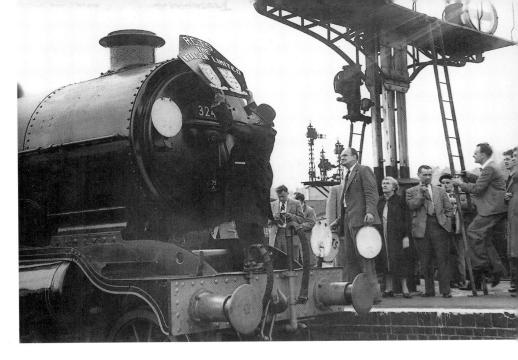

Living on borrowed time, former LBSCR 'H2' Atlantic No 32426 *St Alban's Head* dating from 1911/2 pauses at Lewes on 14 August 1955 with the RCTS 'The Wealden Limited'.
Sussex Express & County Herald

When considering boat trains run on Southern lines, one tends to regard Dover, Folkestone and Southampton as the obvious destinations. However, to do so is to overlook a number of other ports to which such services operated, one such being Newhaven Harbour, where Atlantic No 2424 *Beachy Head* is seen after arriving from Victoria in August 1938.
C. C. B. Herbert

A delightful mixed working once commonplace but rarely photographed. The flat vehicles are 'carriage trucks', upon which the private horse carriages could be conveyed. The assembly was vacuum-braked, hence its inclusion in a passenger working, with 'E4' 0-6-2T No 2503 in charge. The location is recorded as Newhaven Town, but the date is unknown.
Tony Sedgwick collection

Busy times at Oxted in September 1948 with 'D1' 0-4-2T No 2253, 'D1' 4-4-0 No 1494 and 'Q' 0-6-0 No 540, all three engines still displaying their pre-nationalisation livery. Oxted was served by a steam service direct from Victoria, which was a hard duty for the crews. *E. R. Wethersett*

Right:
Road and rail: an unidentified ex-LBSCR Class E6 0-6-2T running cautiously towards Deptford Wharf. *Tony Sedgwick collection*

As a comparison with the earlier view of the 'P' class, here is an example of the 'Terriers'; either type would be dwarfed by almost any neighbouring vehicle. The location is not formally recorded, although it may well be the terminus of the Hayling Island branch, on which route No 32646 was a regular performer for many years. *Hunnard-Morris*

Midhurst in West Sussex once boasted connections to the west, south and east, the result of promoters' competition to reach the town with the railway in the 19th century. Sadly this early enthusiasm was never matched by receipts; 'E4' 0-6-2T No 32464 on the 11.55 'freight' from Midhurst to Petersfield on 4 February 1955 typifies the limited goods service then so common on this and other lines. *S. C. Nash*

Clapham Junction

Mixed liveries at Clapham Junction in October 1948, with 'M7' class 0-4-4T No 30132 coupled to 'E4' 0-6-2T No 32493 on an empty-stock working. *J. L. Smith / Tony Sedgwick collection*

Also at Clapham Junction but this time some years later in August 1960, 'U1' class 2-6-0 No 31895 and 'Battle of Britain' 4-6-2 No 34086 *219 Squadron* wait at the signal with an 18-coach empty-stock working from Oakley Junction to Lewes, running via Tulse Hill. *J. Scrace*

Away from the main line again, to the backwaters of the Isle of Wight, which railway system continued its unique way of life even after the Grouping. The strip of water separating the island from the mainland meant antiquated stock would remain in service long after similar vehicles had been superseded elsewhere, as exemplified by former LBSCR 'Terrier' No 40 *Brighton* with a train of 19th-century stock at Newport. The engine had been sold out of service to the Isle of Wight Central Railway in 1902 as No 11 and came into Southern ownership with the Grouping of 1923.
H. Gordon Tidey /Tony Sedgwick collection

On the Isle of Wight

Even more antiquated was the little Freshwater, Yarmouth & Newport Railway, whose single route served the sparsely populated area west of Newport.
With limited revenue, investment was understandably lacking. FY&N No 1, seen leaving Newport with stock of uncertain origin, was built by Manning, Wardle & Co in 1902 and would be withdrawn in 1932.
H. J. Patterson Rutherford/
Tony Sedgwick collection

Above left:
The 'O2' class, illustrated on page 5, as with all IoW locomotives used Westinghouse air braking, and the pumps required gave the locomotives a unique appearance, as shown in this view at Ventnor in 1965. *M. Dunnett*

Above
The lightly loaded branches off the main Isle of Wight system made an ideal home for members of the 'A1X' class. No 8 *Freshwater* is depicted near Merstone station on the Ventnor West branch in June 1945. *E. R. Wethersett*

Left:
At one time the Isle of Wight had several classes of tank engine to work its services, although steam finished with the 'O2s' working all trains. Before withdrawal, the four former Brighton 'E1' tanks were regularly seen on Island services, the engines in question renumbered in the unique Island scheme. This is No 4 *Wroxall*, depicted at Newport on 1 May 1958. *Ian Allan Library*

Right:
The rural charm of Ventnor West on the former Isle of Wight Central Railway, recorded in its last few years of existence. There were two stations at Ventnor, at vastly differing levels, although both are now but a memory. Ventnor West, formerly Ventnor Town, was the nearer to sea level but further from the town. Here No W8, a 'Terrier' tank, propels the 5.57pm Merstone service away from the station on 18 April 1949.
J. H. Aston

Superpower at Fareham on 15 June 1953 in connection with the Royal Fleet Review in Coronation Year. The engines were stabled at Fareham prior to working back light to Gosport and returning with passenger trains from Gosport to Victoria. Regrettably not all locomotive details were recorded, although amongst the line-up are 'U1' class 2-6-0 No 31903 and 'K' class 2-6-0 No 32349. *Tony Sedgwick*

Around the South Western Section

'T9' 4-4-0 No 30707 is in charge of an eastbound parcels train near Fareham on 20 February 1961. This was the last year that the final survivors of the class would see service, although fortunately one example (No 30120) was saved for preservation as part of the National Collection. *D. E. Esau*

Rural Hampshire: 'L' class 4-4-0 No 31778 has just passed over and exploded a detonator near Bursledon on 23 March 1952. The warning was for single-line working which was operating just ahead, the hand-signalman being Mr Sedgwick Senior. *Tony Sedgwick*

Still on the coast line, this time on the then non-electrified section between Fareham and Southampton, 'T9' No 30287 is seen near Swanwick with a Portsmouth-bound train which appears to consist mainly of Bulleid stock. *P. B. Whitehouse*

'Movement of Army Stores' states the caption on the back of the photograph, but when and where? Southern days for certain, and possibly from the Thornycroft factory near Basingstoke on a section of the Basingstoke & Alton Light Railway. The engine is ex-LSWR 'O2', No 195. *Ian Allan Library*

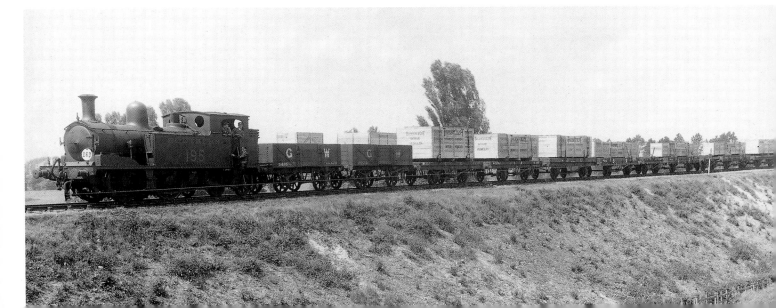

Working hard on the 1-in-60 climb to Medstead on the Alton–Winchester line is 'M7', No 109, at the head of a local service. Notice the pipework for auto working at the front. The crew appear to have left Alton station in a hurry, as the filler-cap on the water-tank is still open. *E. C. Griffith*

The line from Andover to Romsey was a sad casualty of the Beeching axe, dieselisation in its final years being insufficient to save it from closure. Originally it had seen through trains from Cheltenham via the MSWJ route, but these also ceased with the closure of that line in 1961. Just prior to dieselisation 'T9' 4-4-0 No 30732 pauses at Mottisfont station on its way south to Romsey in November 1957. *C. Gammell*

Awaiting the 'off' at Waterloo, 'West Country' No 34012 *Launceston* (right) and another, unidentified Pacific stand at the platform end on 12 May 1965. The figure in the centre is probably the guard of one of the trains, who will have recorded the engine number in his journal and will give the train formation and weight to the driver prior to departure. *Ian Allan Library*

Left:
The little-known Ampress Works Halt, near Lymington, was established primarily to serve a nearby industrial estate. 'M7' class 0-4-4T No 30481 passes with a service for Brockenhurst, in the type's final days of operation on the Lymington branch.
J. S. Gilks

Another Waterloo departure, this time in June 1967, just a few weeks before the end of SR steam. 'West Country' Pacific No 34025 *Whimple* has lost its nameplates (removed legally or illegally, who knows?); the headcode indicates a Bournemouth-line service, although 'SPL' on one of the discs is perhaps not strictly accurate.
Ian Allan Library

Away from Waterloo, although still within the suburban area, 'Q1' No 33018 heads a down freight at Raynes Park on 25 June 1965. *M. S. Stokes*

Until the mass introduction of the BR Standard classes and the cascading of locomotives westwards following electrification on the South Eastern, a number of the former LBSCR 4-4-2 and 4-6-0 designs were regularly seen working the coastway services west from Brighton and also the stopping services between Waterloo and Basingstoke. Here No 32329 *Stephenson* nears Farnborough with one of the latter on 21 September 1950. *G. J. Jefferson*

Farnborough main line in 1963 and 'U' class 2-6-0 No 31635 on a stopping service to Salisbury. Stopping services between Waterloo and Basingstoke passed directly from steam to electric operation in December 1966, with no intermediate diesel era. Diesels would, however, work west of Basingstoke, and, despite mutterings over the years, extension of the electric service to Salisbury remains a remote prospect, even today.
Brian Haresnape

Hardly an effort for 'S15' class 4-6-0 No 30505, as an open wagon, two coaches and a brake van make their way east at Worting Junction, near Basingstoke, in May 1960. With the coaches (at least) being condemned the train required the services of a brake van. *Derek Cross*

The other side of Worting Junction and the climb up to Battledown Flyover from the south, where the up Bournemouth line crosses over the West of England route. This time the engine would probably be somewhat 'winded' from its exertions on the long drag up from Eastleigh, and the crew are no doubt looking forward to a brief respite to Basingstoke. The train is a through working from Portsmouth to the London Midland Region via Reading and Oxford in 1951. Unusually, perhaps, it is hauled by 'L12' 4-4-0 No 30427 of 1904 vintage, most cross-country workings of this era being handled by the larger 'King Arthur' class engines. *E. D. Bruton*

A final view of the area around Worting Junction, as 'Merchant Navy' Pacific No 35021 *New Zealand Line* leans to the curve on the West of England route heading for Salisbury and Exeter on 8 September 1952. Although still in original condition, the locomotive is coupled to the first 6,000gal tender (T3342) to be cut down in the form shown here. This tender was first paired with No 35021 (in February 1952) and eventually survived to be preserved behind No 35028. Sadly, however, No 35021 would meet the cutter's torch, ready to be recycled in a new and unidentifiable form. *Brian Morrison*

The fireman's-side view from the footplate of No 30853 *Sir Richard Grenville* between Basingstoke and Micheldever. From this point to Eastleigh (almost 17 miles) the line falls steadily and is devoid of any sharp curves — small wonder, then, that this was the stretch where a number of the unofficial 'tons' were achieved over the years. *S. C. Townroe*

An April 1953 view of Micheldever storage sidings, which at the time were used for stock that was either condemned or awaiting entry to Eastleigh Works. The deep cutting here had been hewn over the years by the railway to provide infill for expansion at Southampton, the space created being put to good use, as seen. Part of the site was later given over to fuel storage, although the former siding area has for some years now been derelict. *R. H. Clark / Tony Sedgwick collection*

Winchester (City) in June 1966, as No 34019 *Bideford* arrives on a Waterloo–Southampton Central working. Already the conductor rail is in place on the up line, whilst the mechanically operated ground signals would disappear before the end of the year. The steel girders in the yard were from the local firm of Condors, which for many years sent trainloads of steel from the area. *Brian Jackson*

On 29 March 1967 'USA' 0-6-0T No 30064 heads a trip working of mixed freight vehicles trundling across the ladder-crossing from the south yard in the direction of the east yard at Eastleigh. By this late stage of the steam era, the 'USAs' were the last surviving ex-SR tank engines and were to be seen away from their traditional haunt of Southampton Docks, whence they had latterly been displaced by diesel shunters. *J. Scrace*

A 'King Arthur' relegated to freight work, perhaps because the engine in question was run-down and hardly suited to fast main-line working. The location is clearly Eastleigh, the photograph taken from Campbell Road bridge, with a local Hants & Dorset bus ascending the grade. No 30783 *Sir Gillemere* was one of the Maunsell-designed, SR-built variants and is seen attached to at least 26 vehicles on 1 August 1957. *R. A. Panting*

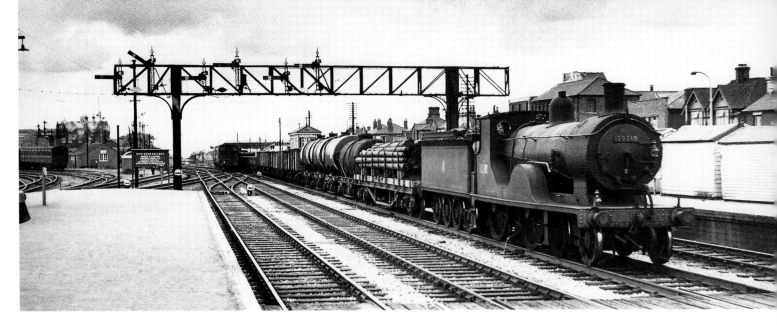

A final Eastleigh view, taken on 13 May 1958 from the down platform, of 'T9' No 30310 on an up mixed freight, probably heading towards the yard at the north end of the station for stabling and reforming. Most freight trains were similarly dealt with at Eastleigh, the yards busy 24 hours a day and also used as the changeover point for both locomotives and crews.
Brian Morrison

Southampton Central, where an unidentified but absolutely filthy Pacific completes taking water prior to continuing on its journey west to Bournemouth. Although the days of steam — and the associated Bulleid locomotive-hauled coaches — were numbered, the mechanical signalling here would continue for several more years, not being replaced until the late 1970s. The cranes in the background are part of the Western (or New) Docks, containers accounting for much of the traffic handled here in later years.
Rod Hoyle

Modernisation at Southampton Docks in 1947: two of the former LSWR 'B4' class 0-4-0T locomotives, Nos 93 *St Malo* and 81 *Jersey*, with one of their replacements, 'USA' class 0-6-0T No 67, in the background. *F. Moss*

Always keen to promote its activities, in the 1920s the Southern Railway released this publicity photograph depicting the 5.50pm meat special preparing to leave Southampton Docks; running at 'express speed', the train was timed for an 8.17pm arrival at Nine Elms. The official caption also pointed out that the train was composed entirely of insulated containers. The locomotive is 'S15' No E524. *Ian Allan Library*

Steam shunting in Southampton Docks, with the driver receiving his instructions via radio — note the aerial on the side of the cab. Such technology seems hardly appropriate to the steam age (and was indeed considered very modern for the day), yet it was a complete success for the short time it was employed on the 'USA' tanks — proof, if such were needed, that old and new technology could work together in harmony. *Ian Allan Library*

Moving west now to Bournemouth Central, where 'U' class 2-6-0 No 31802 — a rebuild of one of the 'River' class tank engines — waits on one of the through roads with the stock from the 9.5am service from Reading General. At the time the photograph was taken — 1957 — there was press speculation that the station would be rebuilt with four platform faces, although, in the event, this did not happen, and the overall roof remains today. Modernisation has taken its toll, however, in the form of considerable track rationalisation. *C. P. Boocock*

The other station at Bournemouth, Bournemouth West, where an unidentified Light Pacific waits at the buffer-stops after arrival. Interestingly there is still a considerable quantity of coal visible in the tender, which seems to dispel slightly the suggestion that this design of engine was heavy on fuel; it could, of course, be that this was only a local service from Southampton or Weymouth.
Ian Allan Library

Poole station in 1964, with one of the hateful level crossings that caused severe delays to road traffic until replaced. The train approaching, hauled by Class U 2-6-0 No 31632, is a working from Brockenhurst via Ringwood, which line would close shortly afterwards. Alongside, at the head of a Weymouth–Bournemouth service, is BR Class 5 4-6-0 No 73041, destined to outlive the Southern type and survive almost to the end of steam. *A. W. Smith*

Double-heading at Weymouth: 'Q' class 0-6-0 No 30536 assists 'N15' No 30763 *Sir Bors de Ganis* out of Weymouth towards Bournemouth in August 1958. The line from Weymouth included a long, steep climb through Bincombe Tunnel almost as far as Dorchester — none too easy for locomotive and crew starting 'cold' from the terminus — and the assistance of the pilot engine, perhaps working back to its home shed, would have been much appreciated. *J. B. Bucknall*

The high-pitched boiler instantly identifies this 4-4-0 as a Drummond 'D15', one of a class of 10 engines built in 1912. Their 6ft 7in driving wheels were similar to those of the 'T9' class, although the 'D15s' possessed slightly larger cylinders and were thus slightly more powerful. Unfortunately the demands of ever-increasing train weights meant their time on front-line duties was limited, and they lasted on secondary duties until withdrawn by BR in the early 1950s. Nearing the end of its days, No 30471 is seen at the east end of Salisbury station. *Ian Allan Library*

Another Salisbury view, this time at the opposite end of the station and alongside the former Great Western signalbox. Brighton-built 'E4' No 32506 is coupled to an ex-GWR shunter's truck and thus possibly employed on a transfer between yards. Originally named *Catherington*, this locomotive was built in 1900 and would be withdrawn in June 1961. *Tony Sedgwick collection*

Approaching Salisbury on 13 September 1958 with an up West of England service is unrebuilt 'Battle of Britain' Pacific No 34062 *17 Squadron*. Again, the GWR signalbox can just be seen on the right, with the flat-roofed Southern 'box in the distance on the left. The GWR and SR had independent routes west as far as Wilton, where the GWR line curved northwest towards Westbury. The crew in the foreground are making their way towards the steam shed, out of shot to the left of the picture. *Stephenson Locomotive Society*

The headcode of one disc in the centre top and bottom instantly identifies this as a West of England working. Class U No 31793 and Class N No 31414 arrive at Semley with a Salisbury–Yeovil service in the summer of 1958. *Ivo Peters*

Bulleid Pacifics on freight were occasionally seen on the West of England line and its associated workings, although the appearance of 'Merchant Navy' No 35003 *Royal Mail* was perhaps still a little unusual and was possibly the result of an unbalanced working. Along with the rest of the class, No 35003 would later be completely rebuilt by British Railways in an attempt remove the eccentricities of the original design and in its modified form survived to the very end of steam in July 1967. *W. Vaughan-Jenkins / Tony Sedgwick collection*

Seaton Junction, with 'U' class 2-6-0 No 31632 running through with an up freight. At intervals between Salisbury and Exeter the Southern installed passing-loops into which slower services could be diverted to allow for through running yet avoid unnecessary delays to faster trains on its principal main line. *D. I. Wood*

The 'M7' class had been designed for a variety of roles, including suburban workings, shunting and, as here, branch-line duties. No 46 is seen with an ex-LSWR 'gated' set near Colyford in 1939. *Tony Sedgwick collection*

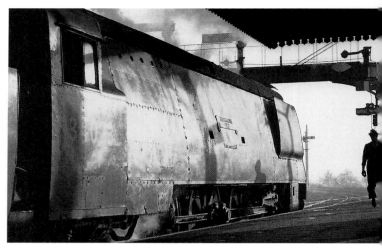

Scenery vans being shunted at Exeter Central in the mid-1930s by one of the larger 0-4-4 tanks, 'M7' No E328. *Tony Sedgwick collection*

From Exeter St Davids, trains for London would depart in opposite directions, depending upon whether they were running via GWR or SR metals. The SR line immediately curved sharply east and began a cruel climb of 1 in 36 to Exeter Central. Caught by late-evening sunshine, No 34023 *Blackmore Vale* prepares to tackle the curve and gradient. *Ian Allan Library*

The same location, but this time viewed from the station footbridge and somewhat earlier in the day. 'Battle of Britain' Pacific No 34056 *Croydon* waits to 'turn left' on a Plymouth–Brighton through working on 23 July 1962. Straight ahead, the GWR line continued along the bank of the Exe estuary to reach Plymouth; SR crews regularly worked trains over this line to retain route knowledge in case of emergency. *Ian Allan Library*

Due to the severe gradient for eastbound SR services leaving Exeter St Davids, it was necessary for most services to be banked between the two Exeter stations. For many years heavy services were banked by the 'Z' class 0-8-0Ts, a train of stone from Meldon being seen here with No 30955 assisting at the rear and No 30956 at the front; the train engine is a BR Class 4 tank, No 80036. The scene was recorded at 1.15pm on 23 July 1962. *Ian Allan Library*

Another Bulleid Light Pacific, 'Battle of Britain' No 34083 *605 Squadron*, shunts the yard at Eggesford, on the line from Exeter to Barnstaple, prior to hauling the 3.25pm Barnstaple Junction–Feltham goods on 5 June 1964. *Ian Allan Library*

Another view on the 'Withered Arm' west of Exeter, this time of the station at Mortehoe & Woolacombe, summit of the line from Barnstaple to Ilfracombe. 'West Country' No 34022, appropriately named *Exmoor*, enters the station on a local working in September 1953. *Ian Allan Library*.

A wet Devon day is in store for the passengers of the 12.58pm from Padstow as it leaves Halwill Junction behind Class N 2-6-0 No 31845 on 14 May 1963. Services on this route would outlive steam in the west country, but only by a short time, as all passenger workings to/from Padstow via Okehampton would cease in October 1966. *Ian Allan Library*

Halwill Junction (or, to be more accurate, Halwill for Beaworthy) again, this time on a dry day. The crew of 'N' class 2-6-0 No 31838 are keeping a careful look-out as they enter the station with the 1.5pm Padstow–Okehampton on 17 August 1963. Halwill was the point of divergence of the Padstow, Bude and Torrington lines, the latter being visible on the left of the picture. *P. Paye*

The scene at Wadebridge, viewed from the driver's cab of No 30587, one of the three surviving Beattie well tanks, which remained in service until 1962 for operating the Wenford Bridge branch. *Stephenson Locomotive Society*

The remains of the Lee Moor Tramway crossing at Laira Junction, Plymouth, on 27 August 1961. 'West Country'
No 34108 *Wincanton* is in the process of turning on the triangle of lines. Southern engine types could reach Plymouth
either via the LSWR route through Tavistock or along the former GWR main line, this particular engine having arrived via
the former. *R. C. Riley*

By way of a contrast with the previous
picture, 'West Country' No 34030
Watersmeet hugs the sea wall near
Teignmouth on the GWR main line
between Exeter and Plymouth, regular
workings of this type taking place to
maintain crew route knowledge. However,
this was not a popular measure with all of
the Southern crews, faced with stiff climbs
west of Newton Abbot to which the Bulleid
Pacifics, with their slipping characteristics,
were hardly suited. *Stephenson Locomotive
Society*

Through workings between the Regions
would often involve a rake of carriages'
traversing almost the length of the country,
even if the locomotive in charge was
changed several times *en route*. One such
example was the Birkenhead–Margate
train, seen here composed of Western
Region stock but with Southern Mogul
No 31798 in charge, passing Shalford
Crossing on 1 May 1950. *E. C. Griffith*

Inter-Regional trains

Inter-Regional workings in the 1950s and
'60s saw former Southern engines working
through to Oxford on some services, whilst
Western engines would reach Bournemouth
and Poole with others. For many years the
Southern would use the 'King Arthur' class
4-6-0s, No 30783 *Sir Gillemere* being
depicted heading south at Reading West
Junction on 23 July 1955 with the through
York–Bournemouth train. *C. R. L. Coles*

Following the demise of the 'King
Arthurs', Bulleid Pacifics took over most
of the Reading and Oxford through
workings, including the 'Pines Express',
which had been re-routed away from the
former Somerset & Dorset as a prelude to
that line's closure. 'West Country'
No 34105 *Swanage* was a regular
performer on this service, particularly in
the early 1960s, and is seen here complete
with a smart rake of maroon BR Mk 1
coaches at Reading West *c*1965. *C. J. Blay*

The Southern also inherited the narrow-gauge Lynton & Barnstaple Railway. Sadly its popularity and revenue between the wars were insufficient to satisfy the accountants at Waterloo, and, along with a number of standard-gauge routes controlled by the Southern, it was a casualty of the harsh economic times of the 1930s. With the demise of the route, the locomotives, carriages and rolling stock etc, were disposed of. Baldwin No 762, formerly *Lyn*, is seen under maintainance on the works road at Pilton shed. *Stephenson Locomotive Society*

The Lynton & Barnstaple

Lynton & Barnstaple 2-6-2T No 188 *Lew* at Barnstaple Town. It is still a matter of some regret that Waterloo considered it necessary to close this delightful line, and it is surely to be hoped that those striving to reopen at least part of the line will ultimately be rewarded with success, make it possible once again to enjoy sights such as this. *Ian Allan Library*